WHERE THE
FUZZY MARMOTS GROW

To Bill ~
With thanks for your
great help & support!

Jim Brennan

Where the Fuzzy Marmots Grow
The Rollicking Adventures of Historic Troop 511

First Printing 1998

ISBN 0-9660826-0-5

Library of Congress Catalog Card Number: 98-70073

Good Scout Publishers, Mill Creek, Washington

Printed in the United States of America

This book is not an official publication
of The Boy Scouts of America

WHERE THE
FUZZY MARMOTS GROW

THE ROLLICKING ADVENTURES OF
HISTORIC TROOP 511!

BY JAMES D. BRAMAN

Good Scout Publishers
MILL CREEK, WASHINGTON

ACKNOWLEDGMENTS

My wife Carol, without whose encouragement, support and active help this book would not have been possible. Gloria, Larry and Paul Campbell and Associates, for excellent editing, preparation of proof, and much other support. Mark Ortman of Wise Owl Books, for his advice and guidance all along the way. Robert Lanphear, for the excellent cover and assistance with photographs. Bob Cram, for the illustrations which so well capture the flavor of Troop 511. Bill Gates, Sr. and Daniel J. Evans for their enthusiastic reviews and notes of endorsement. John Sims, Harold Engebretson and Bob Erickson, for loan of photographs and artifacts used in the book and on its cover. Bill Juneau, Assistant Commissioner of Chief Seattle Council, B.S.A., for invaluable assistance.

My brother Bob Braman and Don ("Hacksaw") Haskell, for their helpful reviews. Taylor Fitterer of Bang Printing for great help during the book production process. And going back a bit in time, Bremerton Lions Club for its generous sponsorship of Troop 511, including funding for acquisition of The Bus and of the site of Camp Tahuya.

Sundown Lodge

Dedication

This book is dedicated to my father, J. D. "Dorm" Braman—
successful Bremerton businessman, designer and builder of
our beautiful family home, Grand Master of the local Masonic
Lodge, Bremerton Port Commissioner, Commander U.S. Naval Reserve, Seattle City Councilman, Mayor of the City of
Seattle, Assistant Secretary of the U. S. Department of Transportation, President of the Chief Seattle Area Council of the
Boy Scouts . . . and arguably the best darn Scoutmaster in the
history of the Boy Scouts of America!

Contents

WHERE THE FUZZY MARMOTS GROW
by James D. Braman

Foreword

What a wonderful power the number 511 has for me! Every
now and then I see "511" . . . sometimes on the digital clock in
the Buick while I'm contemplating life in one of Seattle's
notorious traffic jams. Sometimes on the register in a super-
market checkout line. Sometimes as a page number on a novel.
A time or two as a flight number in the crush of a modern
airport. But wherever it pops up, this number transports me
back in time more than 50 years . . . to a world of green forests, soaring mountains, log cabins, crackling campfires, and
endless exuberance. It always brings a smile and lifts me out
of the realities of the adult world into that world of long ago.

Five-eleven . . . 511 . . . the designation of a Boy Scout troop
in my home town of Bremerton. But surely more than just a
Boy Scout troop! Surely a group of kids and leaders sharing a
special kind of chemistry, brought together at one of those
turning-points in history—those days just before our lives were
changed forever by Pearl Harbor—and at a wonderful corner
of our planet where scouting dreams are perhaps easier to ful-
fill than in most places: the Pacific Northwest.

Now, at last, I write of the memories that after all these years
remain so precious to me. Memories of Bud and Billy and
Johnny, of Dan and Hack and Pete, and of so many others. I
have not attempted to write a history of Boy Scout Troop 511.
Rather, I have put down personal memories of a time that had
such an influence on my life and on the lives of my fellow
Scouters. Memories are just that—memories—and they may

11

be flawed in detail here and there. But the essence is fresh and, I'm certain, correct. I hope these recollections will help you to treasure your own special memories and will make clear why Troop 511—and its scoutmaster Dorm Braman—was a positive lifelong influence for scores of men.

Chapter 1

Chapter 1

OF ZOMBIES AND MARMOTS

The Secret Club . . . Preparation!

I couldn't move. Worse, I couldn't even see! I struggled against the grasp of those holding me, but to no avail. The only sound was a quiet and sinister laugh. Who was doing this to me? Curse that blindfold! My scalp prickled as I felt something slimy and wet slither across my cheek. Then the thing crawled down my sweating face to my chin. No, it wasn't a "thing"; it was several things, wriggling toward my mouth. A stern female voice said, "Open up, Jimmy Braman . . . you know it's decreed that you must eat these worms." I gagged but forced my jaws open.

Then they were on my tongue. Nausea swept over me, but I made myself bite and begin to chew, holding my breath in the hope that I'd taste nothing. Suddenly light flooded my eyes as the blindfold was rudely jerked away. There was a roar of laughter. I blinked to adjust my eyes to the light. Then I saw that the "worms" were only strands of cold, clammy, cooked spaghetti! "Welcome to the Arcana Club, Jimmy!" declared the female voice that I now recognized as my mother's. My own mother! My mother was responsible for all this! But, at least, the Arcana Club initiation ceremony was over.

Arcana Club—she found the name in a dictionary; in Greek "Arcana" meant secret, or roughly so. She had seen that my brother and I, and a small passel of neighborhood boys, needed some activity to help fill their pre-Boy Scout years. A boy had to be twelve to be a Boy Scout in those days, and Cub

Scouting hadn't yet reached Bremerton. So she dreamed up the secret club that met weekly at our house. We did spooky things, played games, read aloud and ate—mom's goodies may have been the strongest force for keeping the club together. To prepare us for the outdoor life of the Scouts she took us on Saturday hikes. One incident from these jaunts was memorable. We had started a campfire and were heating lunch—a large can of pork and beans—in the coals. With a blast that almost could be heard back in Bremerton, the can—unopened in any manner—exploded from pressure of built-up steam. No one was hurt, but it was a hungry (and wiser) group that trailed back into town that summer afternoon!

The Arcana Club certainly filled its niche . . . and was a tribute to a wise and imaginative woman. The "worms," for example, were but part of a special initiation ceremony containing other equally imaginative steps. However, Arcana was, in the final analysis, a prelude to the bigger adventure of membership in THE BOY SCOUTS . . . and, specifically, Troop 511. So, at this point, we bid farewell to my mother, although she always was in the background of our scouting activities, supporting, providing cookies, cleaning up after troop staff meetings.

So To The REAL BOY SCOUTS

My father was known as "Dorm" or "J. D." to the boys of the neighborhood. Most townspeople knew him as J. D. "Dorm" Braman, a loving husband and father and a self-made businessman and civic leader in Bremerton. This viewpoint, however, was subordinated on Thursday nights and many weekends to his position as Scoutmaster of Troop 511. Here he became to some troop members a sort of surrogate father and to all an inspirer, a taskmaster, a mentor, and a friend. I can honestly point out that to some of his contemporary Scoutmasters of other troops in the Bremerton area he was somewhat of a nemesis, a strong leader who was hard to emulate.

No small part of Dorm's success as a scoutmaster and the lively spirit of Troop 5ll can be credited to his Assistant Scoutmaster, Bill Juneau. And fate also presented to the Troop a most unusual and wonderful group of kids. These points will become apparent as my memories unfold.

Dorm showed his dedication to youth by the fact that two years prior to my becoming eligible for the Scouts at the age of 12 (and four years prior to my younger brother Bob's eligibility), he became chairman of the Troop Committee. Such committees customarily are composed of dads of troop members, but he accepted the position at the request of the Bremerton Lions Club, troop sponsors. In short order, he became a sort of de facto Scoutmaster and often led the troop on weekend camping trips. He officially became Scoutmaster after a couple of years' service on the Troop Committee.

His early role gave him an excuse to take me along on some of the troop outings at the tender age of 10. It all seemed very natural to me. Of course, I'll never know if my acceptance by the REAL BOY SCOUTS stemmed from the fact that I was a good guy (a reason I certainly didn't question at the time) or that I was Dorm's son! Whatever the reason, a number of weekends with the troop positioned me for a running start when the eagerly awaited twelfth birthday arrived, and I became a REAL BOY SCOUT.

One of those early Scouting weekends started wonderfully but had, for me, a rather inglorious conclusion. The setting was idyllic for a ten-year-old and, as I see in hindsight, for anyone who loved nature. It was Staircase Campground in the Olympic National Forest, in an area which since has earned national park status. The "staircase" was tumbling rapids on the Skokomish River, and these stairs were flanked by a railing of virgin Douglas Fir and Western Red Cedar trees. The ceiling that weekend was clear, deep blue.

I sat by the river dreaming, a habit that has persisted to this day. In the rocks, pools, and eddies alongside the main flow of the river, I saw things that I never really dared share with the other kids. Here on one pool was a small port city, connected by a thread of sand—a major highway to a metropolis along the riverbank. A riverboat—actually a piece of branch I tossed in the pool—was venturing out into the main stream to reach another port under an overhanging branch downstream. I was now the intrepid skipper of that boat, plunging in the waves of the stream and risking all to reach the other port. "Hard starboard, mate, we're heading straight for Deadman's Rock!" and "Full speed ahead. If we don't tear loose from this blasted whirlpool we're done for!" My ships always made it, but some of my imaginary comrades were not so lucky and plunged on down the stream, battered by rocks, swamped by turbulence, never to be heard from again.

The hours passed quickly in this manner and the few tensions or concerns that I had at that tender age melted away minute by minute. The steady, soothing roar of the river was a pleasing barrier that shut out the rest of the world. I never felt closer to the God that I knew was virtually sitting on my shoulder, taking it all in with me. Or perhaps I was finding Him directly in the panorama of nature before me. No matter, I

18

truly experienced heaven in that setting.

Eventually, a call to dinner broke my reverie. I had a good appetite anywhere, but it expanded considerably in the camp environment. "Wow," I exclaimed to myself—"beef stew!" Now I would have enjoyed that stew anywhere. It really was pretty good, but at Staircase it assumed the proportions of a Michelin three-star. . . well, maybe two-star. . . meal. The cuisine was fine and the ambience absolutely unmatched. At meals I shared the camaraderie of the REAL BOY SCOUTS and almost felt like one of them.

Later came perhaps the best time of all . . . the evening camp-fire. Sitting under a canopy of evergreen boughs with stars glittering through, being warmed by blazing logs, and singing the Scout songs—at the time I thought there could be nothing finer. Looking back over more than fifty years, I find I really haven't changed my mind!

Usually one of the last songs, certainly one of my favorites out in the mountains, had words that remain undimmed:

> "I want to wake up in the mountains,
> Where the mountain breezes blow;
> Smell the flapjacks fryin'
> And the socks a-dryin',
> 'Round the campfire's ruddy glow!
>
> "I want to scramble up the rockslides,
> Where the fuzzy marmots grow,
> And slide down from the topsides,
> On the drifts of summer snow!"

That weekend at Staircase offered the chance to do a little scrambling up those rockslides . . . Dorm said we were going to hike to Wagonwheel Lake. His pronouncement brought a few groans and a lot of happy chatter. (The groaners proved to have a better sense of reality than the others!)

I had a mixture of anticipation and dread—anticipation at being on a real hike with REAL BOY SCOUTS and dread because of the note I had seen carved on the trail sign pointing to Wagonwheel Lake. The words "4 miles" had been crudely modified by a weary returnee to read "14 miles," and others had penciled comments like "4 miles . . . straight up" and "Highway to Hell."

Soon after breakfast we were underway . . . and the "straight up" comment instantly became reality. At the start we were in the cool evergreen forest and things went along pretty well, even for someone like me whose head barely came to shoulder height on most of the other kids. All too soon, the trail switchbacked into more open area with only scrubby trees and scraggly brush. The view improved, but the sun began to seem merciless. Funny, here we were in an area noted for cool rainfall and gray skies, yet I felt as if I were crawling across the desert looking for an oasis.

Onward and upward, ever onward and upward . . . surely we must be almost there? Dorm gave us brief rest periods but with admonitions—wise, but unappreciated at the time—not to drink too much nor to lie down flat. My breath came hard and, finally, only with a wheeze and a rasp. The red huckleberries along the way gave a little refreshment, but the effects were momentary. The story of the "little train who could" lurked somewhere in the foggy recesses of thought . . . "I think

I can, I think I can . . . ." I didn't ask for any special stops . . . probably more out of embarrassment than courage . . . but my dad saw the handwriting on the wall. Quietly and quickly, to minimize my humiliation, he scooped me up and I was riding on his shoulders. I glanced about to see the reaction of the others . . . but they seemed to pay no attention. At the time I thought they were embarrassed for me, but, in later years, I realized that they were too "pooped" to care.

Reluctantly, I found myself thinking, "The view is much better from up here," more because sweat no longer blinded my eyes than from the added elevation. Any sense of humiliation was overcome by relief and gratitude for my dad . . . he had never seemed stronger to me as he plodded steadily up the trail with his added burden.

After some undetermined time—sometimes progress on the trail seemed like the change brought to a mountain's form by the grinding of its glaciers—an older boy at the head of the line shouted "Eureka!" My dad dropped me, and I dropped my earlier fatigue. We all rushed up the remaining incline. Suddenly there lay Wagonwheel Lake, glistening in the sun, surrounded by a necklace of forest and backed by a rocky peak. Clearly it was worth every one of the 14 miles (by this time we all had concluded that the amateur sign alterer had a better grasp of truth than the National Forest people who insisted the distance was just 4 miles).

This was a moment I would experience countless times in following years, both in the Boy Scouts and in my adult life—the warm feeling of gratitude and satisfaction at the achievement of a goal. Forgotten was the fact that I'd had a little help in reaching this one. I knew—correctly, as time proved—that never again would I have to ride on my dad's shoulders, although his support and encouragement over the years were always important.

I lay on my back, enjoying the view of trees across blue sky, long-tailed dragonflies droning fearsomely, but harmlessly, above my face. Even eating lunch, although welcome, for once took a back seat to enjoyment of nature's embrace. I sensed something new to my ten years—a feeling of looking ahead rather than back. I sensed that this was a beginning, that years of challenging work on mountain trails, capped by a great sense of adventure and grand vistas, stretched ahead. I'm sure that from my youthful viewpoint, I did not realize that a human life was being molded and that Wagonwheel Lake represented a watershed. To quote a saying that became popular many years later, I had some vague feeling that "Today is the first day of the rest of my life."

Strangely, the trail seemed to have shortened for our return hike. And everyone seemed to chatter a lot more. True, pounding downhill was a bit hard on the knees, but the knowledge that dinner wasn't too far away helped lubricate them. With a warm glow of a job well done, the boys whooped into camp in the late afternoon. Dinner was good, but the sleeping bags even better after an early turn-in.

"We Need Water!"

During those early days of the Braman family association with Troop 511, the troop camped regularly—usually once a month except in summer—at a cabin by a little lake in the hills west of Bremerton. I discovered in later years that the proper name of the lake is Tin Mine Lake, but we all knew it then as Scout

Lake. A narrow, rough road led into the lake, but a flat-bed truck from Dorm's millwork business carried the kids there easily enough. The cabin was old but quite large, with an upstairs deck for spreading out the sleeping bags and a stove and tables for eating downstairs. I probably visited the camp only two or three times prior to becoming a REAL BOY SCOUT. One night was memorable—a time when I made a better showing than on the hike to Wagonwheel Lake.

It was dark that night outside the little circle of light cast by lanterns shining out the few windows. The air was still and the moon nearly full. Tall fir trees around the cabin cast eerie shadows. Dinner was long past, and the 20 or so boys present— 511 had not achieved the large size it was to know later—had finished an indoor campfire program of Scout songs.

A voice said, "Hey, we're out of water."

Another agreed, "Oh, oh, we're gonna need some for drinkin' and fixin' breakfast."

Innocent enough comments, or so I thought.

Suddenly, in a offhand way, one of the older boys turned to me and said, "How about it, Jimmy? Could you help out here and get a bucketful for us?"

What was I to say? What else could an 11-year-old—aspiring to be a REAL BOY SCOUT—say but, "Sure." Just like that: "Sure."

Sure, I'd go out in the dark, the kind of dark only seen far from the lights of the city, walk probably one half mile across a logged off area with no trail, dip the bucket in the cool stream that was our only water supply, and make the return walk to the glow of the distant cabin. I recalled the talk of the fellows earlier about the bear someone had seen the previous trip. Still I heard myself saying, "Sure. Where's the bucket?"

So with bucket in one hand and flashlight in the other—how tiny the pool of light cast by that little flashlight!—I ventured forth from the warmth of the cabin into the unknowns of Night! As my eyes adjusted to the dark, ghostly shapes emerged in the moonlight. I looked around and saw threatening forms that the light of day would reveal as only stumps and bushes. It didn't take long to figure that the best course was to keep staring straight ahead, walk in as direct a line as possible, and whistle nonchalantly. True, the whistling was a bit loud to be truly nonchalant, but I thought it might prevent me from disturbing the nightly rest of a bear by stumbling into his nest (or whatever these vicious beasts slept in)!

Luckily, as long as I walked a more-or-less straight course, there was no way to miss the stream. It ran almost at right angles to the path from the cabin.

"You know," I thought, "it's really rather nice out this evening. However, I'd better not dawdle . . . those guys seem to really need this water."

So I found myself hustling along, out of a sense of duty, of course.

I came to the stream in a few minutes, alerted by its gurgling, and dipped the bucket full. I seemed to be trembling a little . . from the chilly night air, no doubt. Luckily, as I turned around,

I could see the distant cabin light which not only provided guidance but also offered a beacon of hope that this journey might end without mishap. As I at last climbed the stairs up to the front porch, I adjusted my face to appear casual, perhaps even a touch bored, and pushed open the door. What a surprise! Everyone was shouting in unison, "Hyas Kloshe, Hyas Kloshe, Hyas Kloshe!"

It was my first exposure to the Seattle area Scouts Indian-based shout of commendation and approval, meaning (so I was later told) "Very good!"

There was more. I found that this had been a test. There was plenty of water in the cabin. The first part of the setup was to see whether or not I would go at all. And then one of the patrol leaders followed me part way to be sure I just didn't walk to the rather swampy lake beside the cabin, fill the bucket there, kill a little time on the porch, and then come in. How could they possibly think I'd do such a thing? As I thought about it, though, I realized that would be pretty clever!

At any rate, I passed the test with flying colors and was accepted as almost a REAL BOY SCOUT. As I learned in later years, it could have been worse . . . I might have been taken on a snipe hunt! More on that subject later. Dorm, my dad and the leader of the gang at Scout Lake that spring weekend, sat silently through the whole thing. He always claimed he had nothing to do with it.

Night of the Living Dead

Thirty years later, Dorm and I returned to Scout Lake . . . tagged then as Tin Mine Lake on the government map. The road in

25

was posted "No trespassing," but we figured that didn't apply to old Scouters on foot whose troop used to "own" the lake. As we approached the site of our old cabin, much was different, and yet a lot was the same, too. We could see that the lake really wasn't much—just a large pond, swampy around the margins. The cabin was gone, of course, but the house that replaced it wasn't a whole lot better.

Apparently the folks there were doing some ranching because on the slope where I had my late night water adventure some rather exotic cattle grazed. When viewed in broad daylight through an adult's eyes, one difference was immediately apparent . . . the trees around the lake had grown larger and the distance out to the little water-supply stream had grown shorter.

One thing was the same: down by the lake was the spooky looking mine-hole. I suppose it gave the lake its present name. We'd always heard that the two old prospect holes by the lake had been tin mines. The lake name now seemed to confirm that story, or possibly the lake received its name from a legend that the holes had been tin mines! No matter, the sight of that old hole, its dark and ominous entrance in the dripping, overgrown hillside suddenly brought back a memory.

"Dad, remember the story you told about the mine and zombies . . . and how the kids reacted?" His smile told me that he indeed remembered . . . and I know that everyone there that memorable night can also clearly recall it.

Dorm was always a great raconteur. His stories weren't lighthearted yarns about his youth or about great times in regular Scouting activities. Anyone approaching a campfire at which Dorm was weaving one of his noted stories would not hear laughter or whispering or the restless shuffling usually associated with Scout-aged boys. No indeed, they would note instead breathless silence, not a sound except Dorm's voice softly unwinding a tale of some unspeakable horror. Oh, he didn't go into the gory details so common in the visual monstrosities kids now see at the cinema or to a slightly lesser extent on the tube. The horror was only hinted at—oh, but how effectively! It sprang into reality in the imagination of each boy.

The real secret to Dorm's success in story telling, and it was a success judging by the clamor each night for him to tell another "ghost" story, was a vivid imagination coupled with an ability to set the story in the locale in which it was being told. Also, his sense of timing (all natural, he'd certainly had no training) was exquisite.

... It was a dark night at Scout Lake, a dark night! About 20 of us were sitting in a tight circle around a fire of pine logs, which were spitting and blazing cheerfully. That day we had tramped three miles or so on an old logging road over to a swamp at the base of Gold Mountain. There we followed a rotting plank path to a mine hole much more impressive than the one by Scout Lake. Clearly this one had amounted to something! The extensive pile of tailings covering the slope below the mine proved that this had truly been a mine, not merely a prospect hole. The eerie swamp, the moss hanging from trees around the mine, the rusting scraps of equipment lying about, all helped create an appropriate background for the story Dorm was about to unfold. As usual, Dorm didn't need a shill.

Voices called out, "Come on, Dorm, give us a story!"

He responded, "Well, fellows, I don't really have what you'd call a story tonight. But you know when we were poking around at that old gold mine today, I did remember some history about it. Quite interesting, really, though you might find it a bit dull."

"No, no, Dorm! Tell us!" everyone responded. The older fellows probably knew it was the lead-in to some wild tale, but we younger ones, who found the night pretty spooky, hoped that perhaps it would just be sort of a history lesson. Faint hope!

As always Dorm started innocently enough, with a little background about the days late in the 1800's when several mines, including the one at Scout Lake, were active. Things were pretty wild and wooly then, he told us, but some semblance of law and order was maintained by the U. S. Marshal's office, operating out of Seattle.

His voice growing quieter, Dorm said, "Strange stories began coming into the county seat at Sidney—that's Port Orchard now . . . this was just before old man Bremer laid out the town of Bremerton. Anyway, there were tales about miners from the area disappearing . . . being there with their buddies at night and just being gone the next morning. Well, these miners were a wandering lot and really no one paid much attention at first. But when the son of a local judge turned up missing, I can tell you, boys, things heated up a bit. Soon the old crank phone at the Seattle marshal's office was ringing enough that some attention had to be paid to the disappearances.

"So the chief sent a Marshal Prescott over to Sidney to see what was going on. He rented a horse and rode the wagon trail up to the head of the bay and on up the Gorst Creek trail

28

where he camped the first night. At the start, he was traveling in deep timber along a trail used by the miners. He passed McKenna Falls and just beyond came to a sight he hadn't expected . . . gleaming silver rails of the new logging railroad. Prescott winced, knowing that the big trees he had passed through were doomed. Most of the good lowland timber on the east side of the Sound had been cut for lumber going out to the world on the big schooners sailing the Sound almost every day. The timber barons were starting to work the Kitsap Peninsula. I'm wandering here a bit, boys, but we all saw the damage done by the logging on our hike today."

This was maybe a bit of hypocrisy, since Dorm owned a thriving millwork business completely dependent on lumber from descendants of these same timber barons, but a story's a story.

"At any rate," he carried on, "by the end of the second day, Marshal Prescott camped right here at this little lake, talking with the nine or ten men looking for tin or manganese at the mines you've seen so much of."

At this bit of local color, we all glanced around into the dark shadows, and we could almost feel the spirits of these past miners. A mood was being woven!

"Well," Dorm said, "Prescott found the men here pretty darn agitated. Over the past two weeks, they had seen two of their buddies disappear. Both seemed sensible men who had talked of continuing on for some time. One was missing on a Tuesday morning and the other the very next day. Both had left their gear behind. Of course, it wasn't much, but it was all they had to their names. The marshal could see that the men were really puzzled and alarmed, in fact, close to panic. He pried a little further and got them to admit that the real source of their worry was the big mine over on Gold Mountain. It seemed that both of the missing men had visited that mine before their disappearance and had been reluctant to talk about the experience."

After a tension-building pause for a long, slow sip of coffee, Dorm continued, "So, early the next morning after a good breakfast with the miners, Marshal Prescott mounted up and, with map in hand, headed off toward the gold mine.

"It was a lot tougher going then, boys. The loggers hadn't gotten this far, and the trail went only part way.

"Beating through the brush took hours. Most of the time the marshal had to walk leading his horse, because of the low limbs on the fir trees. They finally reached Gold Creek down in the little canyon we saw today. I'll tell you it took a long time to cross and climb up the other side! At that point, Prescott picked up a trail along Gold Creek and things went better. He arrived late in the afternoon at the swamp we crossed today. He tied up his horse some distance away and took his rifle and field glasses to a place where he could look across the swamp to the mine.

"He focussed on the bunkhouse. There was a curl of smoke from a rusty tin chimney but no other trace of life. He swung his glasses over to the mine itself. A mine car stood on the tracks at the mine entrance. The tailings below it looked fresh—no gullies had been cut by the heavy rains a few days back. The marshal could tell that the mine was being worked actively, but, after an hour or so of intense looking, he hadn't seen anything moving. He knew that the logical thing would be to go over and knock on the door of the bunkhouse, but some instinct told him, 'Don't!' After all, a lot of men had disappeared around here! Marshal Prescott certainly wasn't a coward, but he had survived a lot of tough times by doing his job with a bit of caution. So he decided to wait until dark.

"It was October, just like now,". . . Dorm paused dramatically, as if he had remembered something important. "In fact, it was just 50 years ago tonight, if I recall rightly. Yes, October 12—Columbus Day—it was this very night! Strange, isn't it?

"Anyway, darkness came pretty early. Prescott didn't want to start a fire and attract attention so he pulled his McIntosh jacket tighter and began a cold, lonely watch.

"He had fine field glasses, and they gave him pretty fair night vision. About an hour after dark his patience was rewarded. Ten or twelve men came shuffling out of the bunkhouse in a strange single file march and entered the mineshaft. They were followed by a small man who gave off a sense of power in his swaggering walk. Pretty soon, lamplight was flickering in the mine and the clink of picks and shovels echoed across the black, swampy water. After a while, two men shuffled out of the mine. The small man, who clearly was the leader, shouted at them, and the men pushed the mine car inside. In a few minutes they pushed it out again, fully loaded, and tipped its contents onto the mine dump. In the next hour, they repeated the process several times. Once, the marshal heard what sounded like a happy cry from the small man.

"Then he thought he heard 'This is it! I'm rich!' But this was followed by cursing and what sounded like demands to work faster.

31

"There was something about the way the workers moved that made the marshal feel as if tiny needles were pricking his arms and legs . . . he tingled all over. Then he saw a good-sized rock drop off the hillside and hit one of the men on his bare head. Wow! The man hardly seemed to notice!

"Prescott had been jittery all along, but he had never felt anything like the cold, growing terror gripping him now. Still he was a marshal and knew his duty. So, when the full moon rose over Gold Mountain, he began to pick his way across the swamp walkway. A howling sound some distance away gave him a start until he realized it was just a wolf or wild dog frenzied by the moon, and he continued on. As he approached within 100 feet of the mine opening, the leader, warned by some hidden sense, came out of the mine.

"Prescott leveled his rifle and called as calmly as he could, 'U. S. Marshal Prescott here. I have you covered. We need to talk.'

"The response was a chilling laugh, tinged, the lawman felt, with hysteria. The dark figure called out in a high, unpleasant voice, 'And I, marshal, am Pierre Tenebres, recently of Haiti and now about to become a rich miner in America! What do you want with me?'

"This was followed by a laugh, but I tell you, fellows, there wasn't a scrap of humor in that laugh!

"The marshal, sensing he was dealing with a madman, spoke carefully. 'I just need to see if you know anything about several men reported missing in this area. Maybe some of them

32

have visited you. Let's talk it over, Tenebres.'

"The marshal's fears were proven right by the Frenchman's response, 'No need to talk, marshal. The men you speak of are here . . . or perhaps I should say . . . ha, ha . . . were here. Have you, my dear marshal, heard of the living dead . . . the zombies? Hah, I see you have! One of many dark secrets I learned in Haiti! Now, now, don't protest that I have killed these men. They were leading miserable, useless lives, and now they are working for a good cause . . . to make me rich!"

"With that, his mirthless smiled faded, and he barked out a command in French. The men. . . .zombies—whatever they were—shuffled single file out of the mine straight toward Prescott. Their eyes looked unfocussed, staring straight ahead; their hands were outstretched toward him; they shuffled forward with no more life than puppets on a string.

"Prescott raised his rifle and shouted 'Halt!' . . .once, then twice . . . but they paid no attention and headed straight for him with their picks raised for attack. Sweat poured off his face in spite of the cold night as he squeezed the trigger . . . again and again. Though he had never believed tales about zombies, he sure remembered what he'd heard about them . . . they were the living dead . . . they couldn't be killed because they were already dead! A force of slaves working for the mad Frenchman, requiring no food, working only at night! These and other thoughts swept through his mind as he fled across the swamp in absolute terror, found his horse, rearing and screaming in panic, and attempted to mount him. The horse threw him off and bolted. Prescott hit his head on a log and all went black.

"A bit later, probably only seconds—he had no sense of time—he came to. For a split second he didn't recall where he was. Then he heard that dreaded shuffling sound and a low moaning. He peered with terror-filled eyes into the darkness, and there he saw them . . . ."

At that moment Dorm looked startled, pointed into the darkness over our shoulders and let a blood-curdling scream ring out over Scout Lake. The effect was electric. We screamed, involuntarily echoing Dorm. Ernie fell backwards off the log he was sitting on, earning the nickname "Jumpy."

I don't remember the end of the story . . . I think the marshal was able to shoot the leader, at which the zombies all reverted to their true dead status, or something just as gruesome, but none of us there that night will ever forget the true climax, when we boys were convinced by Dorm's scream that zombies were right behind us!

Conquering The Arctic

It was time for a midwinter weekend at Scout Lake, and this particular time it really looked like winter in Bremerton! Usually winter meant rain, but, once in awhile, the temperature dipped just enough to change that rain into snow. And the week before our February Scout Lake camping weekend, it snowed . . . and snowed some more! Not the usual bit of slushy mess or icy skim on lawns and roads. No, a real snow . . . 8 or 10 inches of dry stuff right in Bremerton with prospect of a lot more in the hills to the west.

Would this deter Troop 511? Foolish question! Led by Dorm, we prepared for our trip as if it were a transpolar expedition.

Everyone was checked-out for warm clothing, acceptable packs, and decent boots. Two large, galvanized wash tubs with lids were mounted on sturdy sleds. Lightweight food was painstakingly selected for our two-night stay. We left right after school on Friday. It was a 40-minute drive on paved roads to the gravel road that headed uphill toward Scout Lake. We parked beside the paved road, pulled on our packs, and trundled the sledges onto the snowy Scout Lake roadbed.

The late afternoon sun shone brightly, and we were sure we'd have no trouble reaching the cabin in a couple of hours. So what if the snow, twelve inches deep at start, seemed to increase by an inch every 100 feet we moved forward. So what if the hill had somehow become a lot steeper than it was when we drove it last month. So what if the snow crust wasn't heavy enough to support the runners of the sledges or feet of those pulling them. So what if we broke through the crust nearly up to our waists every two or three steps. So what if it was getting colder by the minute as the sun lowered. So what if we didn't make it at all? When search parties came would they find our frozen bodies, or bones picked clean by hungry animals?

That evening we learned we could do a lot if we had to. Step by painful step, we trudged on in that semi-conscious state that often blesses weary trekkers. Darkness fell so we proceeded by flashlight. At least the whiteness of the unbroken snow made it easy to stick to the tree-flanked road! Finally, we could dimly see the cabin across the little lake, and soon we were inside building a fire, cooking dinner, and chattering about the great adventure. You can bet we turned in pretty early that night. Yet we didn't sleep right away. We were kept awake for awhile by the sound of a couple of people skating on the lake. Who were the intrepid explorers that braved the lonely road to Scout Lake? We never knew, though we knew that we had made it easier for them by breaking a trail through the snow.

The twanging of their skates on the ice was rather pleasant as we drifted off into sleep. But when we awakened the next morning and went to the lake, our leaders were shocked to see what thin ice the skaters had been on in the darkness of the night. It was cracked and split where they skated but, luckily, there was no hole telling of a complete breakthrough. Our leaders marked off a safe area with thick ice near the shore, and those of us with old strap-on skates had a fine time that day. The rest enjoyed the usual youthful sports associated with snowfall, made more sweet by the work we had gone through to get there.

Sunday morning brought a welcome surprise. A warm Chinook wind had come up and the snow was disappearing before our eyes without the miserable slush created by warm rain on snow. By the time of afternoon departure, we were able to walk out on bare earth tracks.

That night in Bremerton, many families heard colorful stories of the great Arctic adventures experienced by their brave boys! In contrast with all-too-many Arctic expeditions, we had come through without a single casualty. Surely any reasonable person would credit that to our exceptional strength, courage, and resourcefulness!

Chapter 2

AND AWAY WE GO!

Gypsies

A band of gypsies roamed the state of Washington just before World War II. You have a hard time believing this? Well, this group certainly had the requisite colorful clothing, most notably, the purple and orange kerchiefs around their necks and sashes on which craft and folklore accomplishments were boldly proclaimed in colorful symbols. True, these flamboyant hallmarks and the various rituals practiced by the band were largely confined to a chamber beneath the Baptist Church in Charleston, the old name for the west side of Bremerton. But, indeed, this band did set forth from time to time on what its members referred to as "gypsy tours." Of course, their wagons and caravans looked remarkably like trucks and family automobiles of the period . . . simple, dark-colored, four-door Chevys and Fords and Plymouths, plus a ubiquitous flat-bed truck marked on the door of its driver's side, "Braman Millwork Company."

The group's good-natured shouting and singing, both on the road and in its encampments, must have turned a few heads here and there. But, even if so, the annals of the era fail to note the brief passage through history of these "gypsies." Most of them passed into military life a few short years later and then into building and maintaining a great nation as lawyers, surgeons, businessmen, designers, planners, farmers, engineers, and bankers. But they would always maintain deep inside just a bit of that gypsy life, a legacy of the Gypsy Tours of Troop 511 in 1937 and 1938.

By this time, my 12th birthday had passed, and I had been initiated into 511 as a REAL BOY SCOUT. Over many decades memories fade a bit. Looking back I see not a smooth, continuous flow of events, but many vignettes, with certain things standing out more than others. More than fifty years past, many of my Scouting experiences remain crystal clear; this certainly includes parts of the Gypsy Tours.

The Good Dam Project

The first tour I went on was to Eastern Washington. The capitalization of "Eastern" is deliberate. The state of Washington has two distinct faces—Western Washington, gentle, lush and damp, green of land, often gray of sky—and Eastern Washington, harsher and drier, golden land and, more often, blue sky. Eastsiders have been known to refer to the coastal side of the state as the "green hell," drippy, mossy, and with too many people. Folks from the west look at "East of the Mountains" as a rather quaint backwater where it's bitterly cold in winter and hellishly hot in summer. Nonetheless, there's a lot of traffic both ways across the Cascade Mountain passes by people who must secretly feel that the grass is greener on the other side, at least for a long weekend!

But east or west, the real purpose of the 511 Gypsy Tour to the non-evergreen side of the Evergreen State was to check out progress on the world's largest manmade structure, as it was then billed. (The Mongol hordes, prevented from invading China by the Great Wall, might have argued with that claim.) The structure was Grand Coulee Dam—a project dreamed of by visionaries for decades and promoted strongly by many, including the editor of *The Wenatchee World*, during

40

the 1920s and '30s. Franklin Roosevelt had joined the band-
wagon and the long-dreamed project finally got under way in
1932.

The concept was exciting. During the final stages of the last
Ice Age, a tongue of the Continental Glacier had dammed the
normal course of the Columbia River. The entire river had
been diverted southward, and, when a wall of ice collapsed
far upriver, the water released from a huge lake resulted in a
torrent that carved out the great canyon now known as Grand
Coulee. When the ice dam eventually melted, the river reverted to its old channel, and Grand Coulee became a wide,
cliff-walled, dry canyon. Grand Coulee Dam was to be built
across the Columbia below the mouth of Grand Coulee, where
its bed lay hundreds of feet above the post-Ice Age Columbia
River channel. The dam would create a reservoir more than
100 miles long and would generate low-cost power to revital-
ize the Pacific Northwest economy. Perhaps even more important as it was viewed then, a portion of the electricity generated would be used to pump water up into Grand Coulee
which would be dammed with low structures at each end to
create a 25-mile-long reservoir. Water from this reservoir
would fan out over a parched area through a complex array of
irrigation facilities, and the barren but rich soil would become
a green garden-paradise.

Sure, there were problems. Valuable salmon runs would be
blocked. Areas used from time immemorial by American Indians for fishing and habitat would be flooded. A particularly
beautiful length of wild river, including the dramatic Kettle
Falls, would be buried by water forever.

Still, the project held glittering promise in the eyes of most people, including young Boy Scouts, and was awe-inspiring in its scope. Indeed, time has shown that most of the promises in terms of power and irrigation were eventually fulfilled.

Although boys our age were not usually wrapped up in current events, most of us had some idea about the great construction project under way East of the Mountains. So the prospect of going over to see it was exciting, made more so since most of the kids had never crossed the Cascade divide into Eastern Washington. When Dorm recruited enough dads as drivers for the Gypsy Tour—destination Grand Coulee Dam—the 30 boys in the troop gave a silent cheer. Perhaps they subconsciously felt this was just the beginning. As the dam itself was a symbol of the nation's revival and slow climb out of the Great Depression, so the trip was a mark of 511's emergence as a "coming" troop in the Bremerton area. In both cases, great things lay ahead!

I cannot recall details of the drive itself. I remember the excitement of packing, the departure from our troop meeting place at the Charleston church, and the first night's camp on the shores of Soap Lake at the lower end of Grand Coulee. It was the first camping night for me—and most of the boys— away from Western Washington, and the farthest away from home many of us had ever been. We cooked dinner over an open fire, sang scouting songs, watched the lights of the rather scruffy little town just a couple of blocks away, and bedded down on the hard ground under the starlit sky. People today, even young people, jaded by travel to far away, exotic places and by the slam-bang entertainment of modern electronic media, might not understand the great sense of adventure we felt as we lay under the bejeweled sky. "Think of it, two hundred miles from home, and tomorrow we see the world's greatest dam being built! How can we be so lucky?"

Nothing we had heard or read prepared us for what we saw. From the viewing platform hundreds of feet above the scene of activity we each took it in with eyes wide and minds soaking up everything like sponges. Far below, the swirling, surging Columbia was held back by a temporary coffer dam—impressive in its own right—with one half of the enormous concrete structure rising behind it. Machinery roared and rumbled and hundreds of workers did incomprehensible things as great cranes moved concrete buckets to the site of the next pour. Yes, there were narrated explanations of what was going on. But I most remember the spectacle itself and the thought that behind all this activity there was some sort of plan. Order was emerging from seeming chaos—something, a great something, was emerging. I think it was right at that point that the seed for my personal career was planted—beginning with civil engineering, and later segueing into city planning. The excitement, allure, satisfaction, of both engineering and planning—and can the two be far separated?—deeply affected me.

I've made many trips to Grand Coulee since that time and marveled at the great work and its by-products, but nothing has made an impression matching my first visit with the Scouts.

In all honesty, I must admit to another memory. Nothing so noble or awe-inspiring, but perhaps equally typical of youthful adventure. It was our visit to the huge workers' mess hall. I'm not sure how Dorm pulled off our being able to eat there, but eat we did, elbow to elbow with hundreds, maybe thousands, of hungry dam workers.

When we went in the front door, Bud exclaimed, "Wow! This place is bigger than Roosevelt Field! And look at the piles of grub!"

It surely was the biggest building I'd ever been in to that date. I don't remember the menu, but I do remember the quantity! Everything was served family style, great platters and bowls of food at long tables, each seating perhaps twenty hungry workers—and Boy Scouts! When we emptied one bowl, we quickly found another in its place. I suspect that to many of my Scouting pals the meal, and not the dam itself, was the true trip highlight.

Afterward, as we rolled away in our car and truck caravan, all vehicles lower on their springs than when we pulled up, Charley reached under his jacket and pulled out a whole apple pie. With a smile as wide as the pie pan, he proclaimed that it was for a later snack. Of course, he shouldn't have snitched that pie—Dorm never knew about it—but it added some spice to our great adventure. And, in spite of the huge meal we'd all had, our snack time came less than an hour later. We must have recognized the need to destroy the evidence as quickly as possible!

Bee is Not For Braman

The 1938 Gypsy Tour, also a long weekend jaunt, was destined for another spot that most of the Scouts had only seen pictures of—the ocean! The caravan, again made up of dads' cars and the old Braman Millwork truck, ended up at a little cabin camp at Graylands, south of Grays Harbor and fronting directly on the Pacific Ocean dunes. Dorm got several cabins for himself and Bill Juneau and for the other dads. Patterning our experience at Soap Lake the previous summer, the rest of us slept under little pup tents or out in the open.

The weather that time certainly was glorious as it was, at least in memory, during most of our summer and fall outings— blue sky and sea, warm sunshine with just a hint of fog early in the morning. Our first night sparked a lifelong love of the coast for me. A ceiling of stars, just as in the previous year, but with the background roar of the surf, carried my thoughts to the far corners of the globe. To use a more contemporary phrase, "It just doesn't get any better than this!"

A day of playing in the surf, visiting the lighthouse at Westport, going out on a fishing boat over the swells of the bar, and meals by the shore enhanced the magical feeling. But boys are boys, not long content with such low-energy pleasure. By evening, rumors rippled through our Beaver Patrol. We heard that the Lions were going to raid us while we slept, pull us out of sleeping bags, and generally raise hell with us and our camping gear.

We huddled fiercely. Johnny declared, "They won't get away with it! We'll be ready for "em!"

No one could top the Beavers with Johnny as our leader!

We made critical decisions concerning our defense tactics. Then, as nonchalantly as possible, we went about the task of laying out our defensive positions under Johnny's eye so we wouldn't alert the Lions to the fact that WE WERE READY. In fact, in our fertile imaginations, fueled by the recent annexation of Austria by Adolph Hitler, we visualized the Lion Patrol as being ruthless aggressors on a par with Nazi Germany.

But this time the bad guys weren't going to get away with it!

There was a tingle of excitement in the Beaver camp as the long summer twilight came to an end and Dorm called out, "Time to turn in!"

We hadn't told him of our imminent peril from the Lion-Huns nor of our efforts at self-defense. We were brave soldiers, and not snitches. Our plan was simple: to put our sleeping bags close together with a stretch of open sand between them and the dunes. Then, atop the highest dune, with clear sight lines to the Lion camp—in our minds, the Lion fortress—we would each stand guard for one hour. Each one of us would be a brave sentinel in the dark, willing to sacrifice all to sound the alarm and save the other sleeping Beavers.

The first shift went without event, and Red—the first look-out—shook me awake at 11 p.m. and whispered, "All's well, Jimmy. It's your shift; good luck!"

Mine was the eleven o'clock to midnight shift, considered the time most likely for an enemy attack! I sat atop the dune, shivering slightly from a combination of the cool air and anticipation of coming terror. My eyes adjusted quickly, and, with the starlight from overhead and the lack of other distracting lights, I could plainly see the Lion's lair. Time ground on. Nothing happened. I proudly resisted the temptation to nod off. After all, the fate of a nation—the proud Beaver nation—hung on my courageous devotion to duty.

Suddenly, from Lion-land, I thought I saw a motion. I slipped lower, snuggling down into the dune grass. I stared into the dark, straining my young eyes to their limits. Though I didn't see any movement, my skin crawled. Then it crawled more and more. Suddenly I realized that this was some phenomenon beyond fright. I jumped up, turned the flashlight on myself, and found my body covered with bees. Now I had a reason to be frightened! I began slowly to undress. My efforts were rewarded by a sharp sting on my shoulder, followed by one, two, three more. Still, I had no choice but to slowly shed my bee-infested clothes. When I was down to my skivvies, standing nearly naked in the moonlight, I crept back to my sleeping comrades and startled them awake with my discovery. The news was met with excitement and consternation. At first I felt pleased that everyone was worried about me . . . until I realized that they were concerned that somehow I was "contagious" and that the bees would soon attack them!

Fortunately these bees didn't fly at night; I had merely hunkered down in their nest and they didn't appreciate it. By that time we had made enough noise that all other patrols, including the Lions, knew what was happening and of the danger that lurked in the dark. I inspected myself more thoroughly, with the help of others, and found no more bees. We also searched around enough to be satisfied that none were crawling in the camp, so we all turned in again. Needless to say, there was no guard this time. With the threat of the bees, we knew the Lions weren't about to raid us, if they had ever had any intention of doing so!

As I lay in my sleeping bag trying to sleep, imagination took control over common sense, and I could feel bees crawling on my arms, my legs, my every place. It was a long, long night. Fortunately, the bees didn't find my clothing a happy home, and everything was wearable the next morning.

47

More Dams!

Recently, my wife and I camped at the Skagit. To all the Braman clan, "the Skagit" (pronounced ska-jit), means the town of Newhalem, early headquarters of Seattle City Light's great Skagit River hydroelectric project. Today the town still greatly resembles the place of the 1930s, except for some of the older buildings that have been replaced with lawn and flowers. There is a row of bright new homes for City Light workers, and the town now sits beside the cross-state highway that replaced the wonderful old Skagit River Railway.

Newhalem still lies beside the jade green Skagit River, flowing down from the glacier-girt North Cascade Mountains, glimpses of which can be seen beyond the cliffs of the lesser, but still sizable, mountains framing the little town. Beautiful Ladder Creek Falls, lighted at night, tumbles dramatically down a series of foaming cascades in deep rocky clefts. The adjacent Gorge powerhouse generates electricity for homes and businesses in Seattle some 120 miles away. And the mausoleum of J. D. Ross, beloved father of the City Light project, remains carved in the base of a mossy cliff where he helped bring to reality his dream of a vast hydroelectric system to provide the people of Seattle with abundant, cheap power.

In the late 1920s, City Light began operating public tours of the still-unfolding project. These tours were not only a successful public relations gimmick, they were a lot of fun. Perhaps I should say "are," because thousands of visitors each year still enjoy a shorter, tamer version of the original City Light tour. They still find an all-you-can eat dinner, a trip up the fabled, incline railroad platform, and a cruise on Diablo

Lake. It's a nice package, but old-timers know it's only a pale imitation of the tours of the '20s and '30s.

A number of the kids of Troop 511 can attest to this because, late in the 1930s, they enjoyed a sort of special Gypsy Tour to the Skagit. It started with a drive, like other Gypsy Tours, up to Rockport on the river. There the boys joined a couple hundred other adventurers who had come from Seattle by car or buses run by City Light. Here they climbed aboard cars of the Skagit River Railway, originally built by J. D. Ross and his men to carry workers and supplies into the construction areas at Newhalem and farther upstream. Until several years after World War II, road access up the Skagit stopped a few miles upstream from Rockport, and rails provided the only access farther on to the project.

And what a railroad it was! The passenger cars were old streetcars retired from the streets of Seattle, with hard wooden seats and squealing wheels protesting the many sharp turns of the tracks. The average speed seemed about 15 miles an hour, but no one minded; it just allowed time to appreciate the marvelous views of river, forest, and mountains. This probably was the first railroad trip for all the boys from Bremerton—it certainly was for me—and excitement rose higher as the steam locomotive puffed into Newhalem. We were assigned bunks in whitewashed buildings that just a few years earlier had housed project workers. We walked around town a bit to kill time before the dinner which we had heard exciting things about.

About half an hour before dinner time, the line began to form at Gorge Inn (what an appropriate name!), and you can bet that the 511 gang was near the front. Finally, the doors opened and we streamed in to sit at the long tables that filled the large wooden dining room. The food was served to us just as to the workers: plain, hearty, good and abundant, emphasis on abundant! There were plates of fried steaks, platters of chicken and roast pork, bowls of mashed potatoes with gravy on the side, several types of vegetables, plates piled with bread, slabs of butter, pitchers of coffee and milk, even pickles . . . everything to make a Boy Scout's heart glow and his stomach juices tingle.

It was all done family style, with the platters and bowls passed around. Sharp-eyed waiters prowled the hall, and the moment a platter or bowl showed signs of depletion it was replaced by a new one heaped high with the same food. The cooks, working at huge stoves in the kitchen, seemed to perform miracles of supply. To Depression-era boys this was all a marvel and a delight (O.K.! O.K.! It would be a marvel and delight for boys of any era!), and the adults also didn't seem to mind at all.

Then came dessert: homemade cookies, warm apple pies, bowls filled with huge chunks of vanilla ice cream. All serving pieces were bottomless again, with refills coming as long as near-bursting stomachs could bear it. As the Scouts finally waddled out of Gorge Inn, their main thought was . . . "I wonder what'll be for breakfast?"

Right after dinner, tour participants gathered in the new community building for a slide show and talk about the City Light project, how it had come into being, and what projects were planned for the future. After this there was dancing to recorded music. The Scouts generally shuffled about in embarrassment as they eyed the girls who had come up with their families. My main recollection is wonderment at a popular song of the day which I heard for the first time in Newhalem: the Hut Sut Song. Its memorable words started: "Hut Sut Ralston on a rillarah with a bralla, bralla su-et . . . ." At least that's how it sounded! No wonder it made an impression. No wonder that kids who grew up with such fine music deride the ludicrous lyrics of most contemporary rock and rap music!

After the dance we walked up the path beside Ladder Creek Falls. Colored flood lights and piped music provided a stunning experience. No word is more appropriate than "fairyland" for this magical spot. Reluctantly, we turned in with memories of a great day keeping us awake . . . for a few minutes!

A good sleep in the bunkhouses ended promptly at 6 a.m. when piped-in music blared, "Lazy Mary, Won't You Get Up?" We found there was no escape. Loudspeakers on the cliff behind the town proclaimed the same musical question. But, with breakfast to look forward to, it wasn't hard to get the Scouts up, though there was a bit of grumbling among the adults.

Incredibly, the morning performance at Gorge Inn equalled the evening one. Just about anything the boys had ever enjoyed for breakfast was there, and we felt an obligation to the faithful cooks to at least try it all. Juice, milk, cold cereal, hot oatmeal with real cream (not 1% milk, which hadn't yet been sprung on the public!), homebaked sweet rolls, eggs, bacon, sausage, pancakes, French toast. All of this was laid out, and, again, the quantities were endless. Bracing mountain air helped our appetites rise to the challenge. At least that was as good an excuse as any for the sheer gluttony that took place.

After a short settling-down period, we boarded the railway cars to travel several miles up the narrowing canyon to Diablo Dam, the only one of the three current major concrete dams then completed. This trip was the thrill of our young lives. The train traversed tracks perched high above the plunging river and several times passed through dank tunnels carved into sheer rock faces. Continual screeching of steel wheels on steel tracks attested to the sharp curvatures of this very special railroad. Even now, from the perspective of a lifetime of travel to many of the planet's wonders, I remember this excursion as a world-class experience.

We arrived at the upper camp just below Diablo Dam and briefly visited the powerhouse. The two hundred or so people on the tour were herded onto a broad wooden platform surrounded by a safety fence. Looking up the steep slope above us, we saw widely spaced rails on its face that gave us a pretty clear picture of what lay ahead. With a little lurch the platform began to crawl upwards. This incline railway was not built for tourists. The rail tracks on its deck showed that it served the functional purpose of delivering building materials and supplies via rail car to the upper end of completed Diablo Dam and to the work boats that carried supplies up Diablo Lake to the foot of Ruby Dam. This dam, later renamed Ross Dam in honor of J. D. Ross, was then under construction.

We rode up and up and up. The elevation gain was a nerve-wracking 400 feet. Surely those cables holding our fate were too small to carry such a load! In a couple of minutes, we looked up at the control building and saw the man who operated the controls of the huge wheels that were reeling in the cable. Our lives were in his capable (we hoped!) hands. We arrived with a slight bump at the top, and two large steel hooks dropped into sockets on the deck to secure the platform. Just as two hundred people quietly breathed sighs of relief, the platform lurched and slipped backwards! Was the trip down to be a whole lot faster than the one up, with a thundering, disastrous ending? No, with a clang the movement stopped abruptly. We looked up to see a fiendish grin on the face of the operator. Clearly he had brought the platform up a little higher than the proper stopping position, then let it quickly slip back about half a foot so that the safety hooks bound securely into their sockets!

The boat trip up beautiful Lake Diablo would have been an anti-climax but for the beauty of jade-like water and the majesty of glacier-clad peaks soaring high into the azure sky. As we approached the site of Ruby Dam, which ultimately would tower more than 500 feet above the water, the lake narrowed so that only a few feet of clearance lay on each side of our boat. The officials briefly explained the work going on there and described the great amounts of power that would be generated for Seattle. Then we returned down the incline and boarded the railway for a final lunch—as spectacular as the other two meals at Newhalem. We had seen wonders: the sheer downstream face of the great arching Diablo Dam, the exciting incline trip, the grandeur of the rail trip up the Gorge, and the spectacular beauty of Ladder Creek Falls by day and night. Still, there's little doubt that had a poll of the Scouts been taken, the number one attraction would have been the meals at Gorge Inn!

These Gypsy Tours were but the prelude to the great and final trip in 1939. Where the first ones covered 3-day weekends, the 1939 journey would take two weeks and travel through five states. It deserves a special chapter later.

Chapter 3

TAHUYA

Ousted by the Frogs!

"A frog farm! Some Californian's going to turn Scout Lake into a frog farm?"

If Dorm had announced to the troop that Bud, our Senior Patrol Leader, was going to be married next weekend, the level of incredulity wouldn't have been greater. Were we really going to lose beloved Scout Lake? How could such a disaster occur? The fact of the matter was that the troop had been using the old cabin at the owner's indulgence, and that some Californians had indeed bought the property for use as a frog farm and that we'd have to move on. A frog farm! We thought with disgust that only goofy Californians would farm frogs. We never did find out if anything ever came of the frog farm idea, but the sale of frog legs at Bremerton restaurants—all three of them—showed no increase from its base of zero!

Nonetheless, the sale was real, and it set Dorm into action immediately. Troop 511 must have a camp; camping was the heart and soul of scouting. If we couldn't have Scout Lake we'd have something better!

So began several weekend drives into the Green Mountains west of Bremerton. Scout Lake was set on the edge of these "mountains"—hills by Pacific Northwest standards but exceeding the height of the Catskills and Poconos in the East. These hills extended far beyond that little pond. At least it seemed far when driving through the area on the maze of old logging roads; in truth, the hills probably weren't more than ten or twelve miles across. Dorm, accompanied by me and often one or two of the older Scouts, searched for our new Camelot, although probably none of us had yet heard that term.

It took only two or three trips to find it. Out beyond the little hamlet of Crosby, we found a narrow road, not much more than two tire tracks, and followed it on beyond one last old house to a little river in the deep woods. We crossed the stream on an old log bridge used decades earlier by loggers. Beyond that, we came upon a road junction . . . which way to turn? Dorm chose left, and, in a couple of hundred feet, we broke into a large clearing. This open space appeared to be an abandoned farm. A large, dilapidated, two-story house, with a couple of sagging outbuildings, lay at the far edge of the field. Some moss-crusted fruit trees, pretty much beyond their fruit-bearing life, flanked this old building.

We jumped out of Dorm's truck and poked around the old house. A couple of beer bottles of recent vintage lay about, indicating that we weren't the only explorers who had run across this outpost in the backwoods. Dorm found a door in the floor leading to a dank earth cellar. Down there we discovered rotting shelves and empty bottles full of spider webs—hundreds of bottles. Dorm whistled softly.

"Hey, this is an old moonshiners' hideout. They must have made booze here during Prohibition!"

To us kids that seemed a titillating conclusion—something strangely evil and mysterious, out of the distant past. In fact Prohibition had ended just six years earlier, and illegal brewing and distilling, on a small scale, had been quite common in rural areas. Nonetheless, we had visions, fed by Grade "B" matinees and youthful imagination, of gun battles between federal agents and moonshiners, of wild drunken orgies at this very house.

"Dorm," we excitedly exclaimed, "This would make a great place for our camp."

I think Dorm shared a little of that excitement, but he felt obliged to present a facade of reason.

"Water," he said sagely, "Water's the key to a successful camp-site. They must have had some around here."

So we explored. We found an old well, but it's top was pretty well rotted, and throwing a rock in didn't generate the hoped-for splash. We walked to the edge of the field and through a rim of pine trees. There we came upon a large marsh. At one end there were signs of a failed drainage system. In later years, we learned that a turn-of-the-century farmer had drained the swamp, built the house, and attempted to farm the old marsh bed. His fate we never learned, but clearly the drainage project wasn't successful because nature had reclaimed the area as a full-fledged swamp. But swamp water doesn't make for good drinking!

We retraced our steps across the field and the road. A faint breeze riffled the tops of the pine and fir trees. It was quiet! Did Indians lurk in the dark corners of the forest watching us—bows and tomahawks on alert? Dorm apparently had no such thoughts and pushed ahead on a faint trail. Then we heard a welcome sound—the soft gurgle of water. Suddenly we were on the bank of a stream, the same one we had driven across earlier on the old bridge. Ahead was a little pond where two branches of the stream joined, and the combined flow passed on under arching trees and Northwest underbrush. We had found our water.

Dorm, unknowingly aping Brigham Young as the latter gazed out over the Salt Lake basin about a century earlier, said quietly, "This is the place."

I'm certain that Dorm had to do a great deal before it was actually our place, but the excited kids in Troop 511, as they visited the spot on a later weekend, knew that it was destined to be our new camp site. I recall that Dorm had to persuade our troop sponsor, the Bremerton Lions Club, to come up with two hundred dollars, no mean sum in those late Depression days, to buy the eighty acres. Yes, that's correct; the Lions paid $2.50 per acre for nicely forested land with a year-around stream on it! But before the actual purchase, they had to search county files for ownership records and title information, and take various steps to purchase a piece of land that wasn't posted for sale.

A perusal of old maps showed that the stream was rather grandly called "Tahuya River." It had its source in the rather swampy Lake Tahuya three or four miles away, and eventually flowed as quite a respectable stream into Hood Canal, some twenty airline miles to the southwest. In those days, no one gave a thought to the purity of the water. It was cool, sweet, altogether suitable to slake the thirst and take care of the cleaning needs of a Boy Scout troop. And so it was used by Troop 511 and other Scouters in the years before a well was dug.

Our acquisition of "Camp Tahuya," or just plain "Tahuya" as we always called it (Dorm's official name of "Happy Valley Camp" just didn't take), unleashed a great burst of collective energy. Dorm and assistant Bill Juneau planned and organized a camp-building effort perhaps unmatched by any single troop in the annals of the Boy Scouts of America. They designed a fine big natural log building for the edge of the clearing. Dorm had a natural flair for architecture, having previously designed our family home which still remains a showplace in Bremerton. We began a logging operation on a remote part of our property. Support posts were properly placed on concrete pier blocks, and the building began to emerge. We felled trees by hand, sawed them into proper lengths with two-man crosscut saws, and hand peeled and planed them to the degree necessary using hand-wielded adzes. To supplement the hand-sawing effort, Dorm rigged a large circular saw powered off the rear axle of his truck

Every weekend that summer we staged a big work party at the campsite. Sometimes these were day parties; sometimes we stayed overnight in "Haskell Hall," an old cabin up the hill from the clearing. We deemed this old building to be in better condition—though barely so—than the sagging and dank farmhouse. Haskell Hall, named for one of our troop members who first discovered it, lay at the end of a narrow road in deep woods. It was a rather spooky place and Dorm couldn't resist feeding on this atmosphere. None of us who were present will ever forget the dark spring night that Dorm came forth with one of his "true" stories. As I noted earlier, he was full of them wherever we traveled. None of the boys ever questioned his amazing knowledge of isolated bits of ancient history (to us, that meant more than 25 years back!) in these varied places. To be sure, I can see now that this "knowledge"

59

was mostly a good imagination, but, in those days, we neither knew nor cared about that!

The Haskell Horror

On this particular night, dinner was long finished, the cleanup done, and normal evening horseplay ended. It had been a tiring day of work and we were ready to crawl into our sleeping bags on the hard floor.

Almost ready, that is, until one boy called out, "How about a story, Dorm?"

He was joined by a dozen others.

In his usual fashion, Dorm at first demurred, "Fellows, it's been a long day. I'm sure ready to hit the hay, and I'll bet the rest of you are too!"

He knew how to play his audience! After much clamor, with great apparent reluctance, he finally said, "O.K. O.K. Anything to get you guys quieted down. There is a bit of history about this location you probably should know something about and I guess now is as good a time as any." He thought for a bit, then said, "You know, it's not really a pleasant story and maybe we should skip it . . . ." Of course, he expected the resultant outcry, which he quieted with a big sigh, then he said, "Well, don't anyone say you didn't ask for it."

I pulled my jacket a bit closer about me, to fend off the sudden chill in the air, just as Dorm began speaking.

"Boys, just try to get this picture in your heads. Before the turn of the century most of Kitsap County was covered by huge trees . . . some of you who have been up to Mount Rainier have seen the type of trees that used to be everywhere around here. Timber companies had been working other lowland areas around Puget Sound for thirty, maybe forty years, and had started along Hood Canal several years before the strange events I'm telling about tonight. There was a big sawmill over at Seabeck—it kept operating for a long time before it finally burned down—and a smaller one down at Clifton; that's what Belfair used to be called. You can imagine that working in the woods and in the mills was a pretty lonely existence. There was a network of logging railroads centering on each mill, but almost no roads. The little mosquito fleet steamboats that ran around the Sound—like the Reeves that still goes up to Silverdale—came into the dock at Seabeck, but Clifton didn't even have that link with the world. Because of this, the Saturday night parties were very important—sometimes even local girls joined in." A chorus of groans came from most us, virtually all confirmed woman-haters at that age. "The men from Clifton especially enjoyed spending a weekend once in a while at Seabeck which was a larger and more lively place than their little settlement.

"It wasn't an easy trip. There was a crude wagon road for a few miles, and the rest was a ten-mile trail through the unlogged forest. Seems like a long hike for a little human companionship, but a lot of fellows did it."

"Did the trail go anywhere near here, Dorm?" I heard a small voice ask.

"Well, that's the interesting part," said Dorm, "It passed right along what's now the old road a couple hundred feet north of here, the road we walk down to get to the campsite. Early road builders just followed old trail routes wherever they could."

Dorm stared at the old wood stove which was fending off the night chill although, suspecting a bit of what might lie ahead, some of us shivered anyway. "Well, strange things began to happen during the fall of '94. A treetopper from Clifton decided to go over to Seabeck for the weekend one Friday night in October. You can see it would be a darn spooky walk through the big timber at night but old Swede—really, no one knew if he was Swedish, Norwegian, or whatever, but he was tall and blonde and never kicked about being called Swede. Anyway, old Swede wasn't around Monday morning when the logging crews headed for the woods south of Clifton. Nobody thought too much about it for a day or so, even though the topper was a mighty important man in the operation, and Swede had always been one of the most reliable guys around.

"The foreman was getting pretty upset by Wednesday morning and mentally threatening Swede with dire punishment when he returned, but soon his anger changed to worry. It just wasn't like Swede not to be on the job. So the foreman did something he didn't like one bit; he used the primitive telephone system which linked Clifton to Sidney and Sidney on to Seabeck. Remember that Sidney is what Port Orchard was called then. The connection was pretty darn awful, but, after a few minutes, he was convinced that Swede had never arrived at Seabeck. The foreman let a couple of men who planned to go to Seabeck the next weekend leave a little early on Friday so they could make the trip in daylight and look for a sign of Swede along the trail. When they returned Sunday night, they told everyone that they hadn't seen any trace of old

Swede nor anything unusual along the way.

"Well, fellows, that seemed to be the end of it; it was just assumed that Swede, always an independent cuss even if usually reliable, had decided to take what he had on his back and move on. But the very next weekend the whole thing happened again. This time the operator of the donkey engine disappeared; he reached Seabeck from Clifton all right, but never showed up after leaving for home camp on Sunday evening. Then, in short order, there were two more disappearances . . . one fellow from Seabeck traveling to Clifton and another Clifton man headed for the Seabeck mill on business.

"Believe me, things got mighty tense in this part of Kitsap County when the word got around. The sheriff's office in Sidney was contacted, and a tough young deputy named Moe Springer was sent to Clifton. Moe told folks later he didn't really expect that foul play was involved, since loggers and mill workers didn't have much in the way of roots in any one area, and moving around without notice wasn't out of the ordinary. But when Springer began checking on a couple of the men who had disappeared, he changed his mind. The Seabeck man had a sweetheart in the Clifton area, and everybody knew the two of them were going to be married before Christmas, and, as I mentioned, the missing Clifton man had important mill business in Seabeck—he was a top level guy in the company. It just didn't make sense that either of these men would walk away; Springer decided that something must be wrong for them to be missing.

"So he took along a volunteer from Belfair and made a careful search of the trail between the two camps. He didn't turn up any clues at all . . . in fact, he was surprised at just how far in the backwoods the trail lay. There were only a couple of isolated cabins on the whole length . . . one of them was this place we now call Haskell Hall."

Dorm paused and looked around the room. It was pretty darn dark in there. The one kerosene lantern at his feet cast a feeble light making odd shadows across the faces of the boys near him.

With a sigh that seemed to indicate a reluctance to go on, he said, "Springer was a determined young man. The more he thought about it the more he knew something was wrong and that he had to get to the bottom of it. Then he had a thought. The disappearances had all happened at night, and the men involved were traveling alone. He would have to travel from one camp to the other alone and after dark. He was a brave man, but not a foolhardy one, and he didn't like the idea of making this trip. However, he knew where his duty lay and, besides, he still couldn't quite believe that anything sinister could happen along a trail with little sign of wildlife and almost no habitation. Anyway, he'd be forewarned and armed, and he was sure he could handle anything that might come up.

"So the next night, under an almost full moon, he set off at dusk from Seabeck. A group from Clifton had promised they would meet him at the end of the wagon road early the next morning. He carried a miner's carbide lantern and, along with the moonlight, could see his way well enough along the forested path. After about two miles, he came to the first cabin. He'd planned to stop in for a brief chat, but no one seemed to be around, so he pushed on into deeper forest. The light of his little lantern reflected off the dead squaw wood at the base of

the big evergreen trees, creating ghostly images. A sighing in
the branches sounded as if it came from those missing men,
though Springer knew—didn't he?—that it must be caused by
a faint nighttime breeze. He pulled his heavy jacket closer as
the chill deepened.

"The tension he felt was taking a toll, and Springer was glad
finally to see a faint light off to the side of the trail through the
branches of fir and underbrush. He knew it must be the second cabin that he'd seen on his daytime trip. He searched his
memory and recalled that the County records showed the owner
to be Ivar Swenson, an old recluse. People at the Seabeck mill
said Swenson was sort of a strange duck, but he had never
bothered anyone.

"Springer was anxious for a little human contact, and he also
thought it might be a good idea to talk with Swenson to see if
he could shed any light on the mystery. As he turned up the
little path to the cabin door . . ." (we shuddered as Dorm
paused again) "remember that the cabin is where we're sitting right now—he suddenly felt a chill far beyond that of the
night air. It was like an ice-cold hand had suddenly been placed
on the back of his neck. If he'd never before known the meaning of the words, 'making your scalp crawl' he sure did then!
Springer resisted an impulse to turn and walk—or, better yet—
run away, telling himself he was being foolish. Still, for the
first time, he wished he wasn't a deputy sheriff with a sworn
duty to uphold.

"As he got close to the cabin door, he was startled to hear
voices; either two people were in there or the old man had
gone crazy and was talking to himself! No . . . there definitely
seemed to be different voices: one speaking loudly, you could

65

say hysterically, and the other sort of growling, almost animal-like, ending in a whimpering sound. The deputy screwed up his courage and knocked on the rude wooden door. He could feel the tension inside the cabin flowing out like the Tahuya in flood stage. There were more words, excited ones, and a scrambling inside. Springer instinctively drew his Colt revolver as the door slowly creaked open. The light in the room made it difficult to clearly see the old man before him, but he had no trouble spotting the rifle held at waist level, pointing straight toward Springer's belly.

"Well, fellows, you can bet Springer was scared to death, but there really wasn't anything he could do but carry on. He drew a breath and said, 'Sorry if I've disturbed you, sir. I'm Moe Springer, Deputy Sheriff from Sidney, looking into the disappearance of some men in this area and I . . . .'

"The old man lowered his rifle a bit and spoke, a little too quickly it seemed to Springer, 'Don't know nuthin' about it. Sorry I can't help,' and began to close the door.

"The deputy very, very, carefully pushed his way in and started to explain that he wanted to ask a few questions. Old Swenson flew into a rage, pulled up the rifle, and growled, 'Git outta here. This is my place and I ain't harmed nobody but I soon will if you don't leave me alone so get out and I mean now!'

"The words tumbled out hysterically, and Springer knew for sure he was in great danger. He kept his voice as level as he could and ordered, 'Put down that rifle, Swenson.'

"'How d'ya know my name,' the old man cried wildly, as he pulled the trigger. Instinctively, Springer had just started to jump to one side as the awful blast filled the room. He felt a lance of pain in his left arm and pulled the trigger on his Colt before the old man could get off another shot.

"'What a nightmare,' he thought. 'Can this really be happening.' The old man fell without a sound and, before Springer could break from his trance and move, there was . . . . . ."

A hellish scream filled Haskell Hall and twenty boys gasped as one. Fortunately, none of us healthy young lads suffered from weak hearts! Dorm continued as the trailing edge of his scream faded into absolute, death-like silence.

"Springer's heart pounded to the point of bursting at the scream, and he looked up to see a horrible apparition in the lantern light. Before him stood, or more accurately crouched, a hairy figure with a human-like face. This monstrosity screamed again as he looked at the fallen figure, then broke into whimpering sounds that seemed to be attempts at words. Suddenly, the figure, deep-set eyes afire with hatred, sprang toward Springer. The deputy fired twice and the figure, screaming with pain and anger, fled out the open door.

"Of course, Springer was just about hysterical himself by this time, but he pulled himself together and examined Swenson, who was now stirring and moaning on the floor. Blood was soaking through his jacket. The old man motioned for Springer to lean down and in gasps related a story that no one will find in the official files of the case."

Well, 1938 was long before most of us had heard the term 'mutant,' but Dorm told us the monster that tried to attack Springer was the freak son of old Swenson. For some reason still not known to this date—Dorm said he hoped it had nothing to do with the air or water around Tahuya—the boy as he grew up took on more and more characteristics of an animal.

"Swenson told Springer he'd tried to keep the boy out of trouble and away from public ridicule by bringing him up in the isolated wilderness of Kitsap County where he'd been born."

Dorm continued, "Springer knew deep inside that he was near the answer to the mystery, and he prodded the old man on this point. But just as Swenson was trying to answer, a terrible gurgle arose in his throat, he coughed a couple of times, and Springer could see that he was gone. This was horrible, but worse was to come. He bolted the door against the return of the mutant son—he certainly didn't have the nerve to set out after him in the dark—and began to search the place, holding a rag to the wound in his arm to slow the bleeding. In the next room was evidence that the son was like an animal, a carnivorous one at that. Chunks of flesh and bones from small animals littered the kitchen floor.

"Springer then noted a trap door in the floor—it's the one right over there by the kitchen," Dorm said in a voice not much louder than a whisper. We all knew that door; it led to a dank semi-cellar that was spooky enough even in broad daylight but seemed absolutely terrifying now.

"Springer pulled it open, lowered the lantern, and then, with a wave of faintness and nausea, saw what was below—a pile of bones obviously of human origin! When he saw gleaming faintly at the edge of the spill of lantern light a grinning human skull, Springer slammed the trapdoor shut and sat shuddering, forcing back the bile in his throat.

"Of course that solved the mystery of the missing men," concluded our Scoutmaster.

After a moment of shocked silence, one of the older boys remained bold enough to ask, "And what ever happened to the crazy son?"

Dorm slowly shook his head, took a long sip from the cup of coffee he had been nursing along, and said reluctantly, "Well, boys, he was never seen again. Of course, he was hit by at least one bullet; maybe he died in some part of the forest where his body was never found. But, who knows, he must have been tough as nails and might have survived. Let's see; he'd be about 70 years old now if by any chance he's still alive." Dorm mused, "But where do you suppose a thing like that could live out here—he never knew any place but this old cabin. Of course, there is the cellar down there . . . " Dorm let his voice fade away dramatically as he glanced over at the trap door. Then with a sigh he concluded, "Naw, I doubt he's still around." Then, with a glance at his watch. "Ten o'clock. Time to turn in. We've got a big day working down at the lodge tomorrow."

It was a very long night for twenty of us at Haskell Hall!

Sundown Lodge: Four Stars by Any Standard

The form of the lodge was taking shape. As the impressive peeled log walls rose, so did everyone's excitement and eagerness to get the job done. This was to be no mere cabin. Dimensions of the main room were about twenty-five by forty feet, with an additional kitchen ell. A huge stone fireplace

69

was planned for one end of the main room. The steep shake roof allowed room for a sleeping loft about half the size of the main floor. There would be paned windows with solid plank shutters all around. And for the kitchen, Dorm had scrounged a huge, wood-burning, restaurant-type range from a local hospital that was being remodeled. Bill Juneau used his connections with the Navy Yard to get some old, but sturdy, folding dining tables and benches. Yes, Sundown Lodge, as we christened it, was to be the pride of Kitsap County scouting!

A big challenge remained as the walls approached their full height. We had cut and hand-peeled and adzed the logs from our own property, but where to get the stone for the fireplace and chimney? More explorations were in order, and it didn't take long for Dorm and Bill to find alongside a logging road near Gold Mountain a great outcropping of stone that admirably met our need. The stone was naturally fractured, quite easily broken along relatively flat planes, and handsome in appearance. We loaded the flatbed truck several times for the bumpy five or six mile trip to our campsite.

Dorm had a way of rallying boys and fathers alike, and one dad experienced in masonry spent several arduous weekends laying up the stone for the fireplace and chimney. His skill was shown in the attractive stonework in the massive fireplace and the great varnished log mantelpiece. It was also apparent in the fine way that fires burned with smoke going up the chimney where it belonged and not into the room. The freplace included a heat circulator that heated the huge space pretty well.

Friends of our troop donated a collection of old furniture. Especially memorable was a large overstuffed couch we placed in front of the fireplace. Soon the lodge was completed and pressed into regular service. We made weekend trips to Camp Tahuya once a month, skipping one month each summer when we made our annual mountain hike and when many of us also spent a week at Camp Parsons of the Seattle Area Council, on Hood Canal. In rainy weather, all of the boys slept in the lodge, and we had an occasional meal there. However, we were a tough bunch and the weekends were intended to be camping experiences. So soon after completion of the lodge, each of the five patrols built its own cedar shake shelter (with Dorm serving as a one-man Design Review Board) in locations near the Tahuya River, not far from the lodge. Shelters were open-fronted and not large enough for sleeping—that was done in sleeping bags on the open ground when weather permitted. But the shelters provided storage for food, cooking gear, etc., and a place for preparation of meals over a campfire at the front.

Beaver, Cougar, Eagle, Lion, and Hawk patrols competed fiercely with each other. (Pheasant and Fox patrols were added later as the troop grew.) Each campsite and all patrol members were inspected by Dorm and Bill on Sunday mornings. The site had to be raked and neat, and boys presentable—even hands scrubbed clean. Winning the monthly inspection was a source of pride, and each patrol worked hard for the honor.

The patrols prepared their own menus and did their own cooking. Some efforts were ambitious—sometimes maybe too ambitious! The Beaver Patrol leader, Johnny, once baked a lemon pie buried in a hole lined with hot rocks. He then covered the hole with wet branches and built a fire on the top. Let's just say that the result was a bit on the soggy side, al-

71

though, as I recall, it all was eaten! Overall, results improved as time went along, and some pretty good meals were soon being cooked by the patrols.

The most memorable meals, though, the ones greatly anticipated by the boys, were cooked on the annual Dads' Day when fathers were invited. Nearly all dads came to spend a fall weekend at the camp. Highlights were the boys versus dads softball game, and the dinner cooked by Dorm and Bill. Pan-fried chicken, mashed potatoes and gravy, vegetables, and pies baked in the oven of the huge range were highlights. And what pies those were! Sometimes they were made with the wonderful, little wild mountain blackberries found in the logged-off areas, sometimes with peaches or apples, enclosed in flaky crusts with fragrant juices oozing out. Dads found themselves coming to the annual gathering not just out of duty to their sons, but also to get a first-class meal served in a world-class lodge!

A Fire and a Football Field

While we were building Sundown Lodge, other improvements to the campsite were taking place. Dorm and Bill wisely decided that the old farmhouse and outbuildings provided just too much temptation for play. In their decrepit condition these old structures were not safe. They had to go, and it was a bit sad to see it happen.

One time while exploring the house, I tore off a piece of old wallpaper and underneath found a 1898 San Francisco newspaper. It told of Admiral Dewey's triumphant return to that city with his fleet, fresh from the great victory at Manila Bay. Nothing to that point in my life had made history jump out in such a real fashion. I had some vague understanding that my grandfather had fought and been wounded in Cuba during the Spanish-American War and here was a newspaper recounting a victory in that same war. It really did happen!

Our leaders decided that the most practical way of removing the buildings would be to put them to the torch. So one cool evening after a rainy spell, the fires were lit. Those dry old buildings went up in a firestorm! The raging flames reflected in the eyes of excited boys who had never seen a big fire. This was a fire they could especially enjoy because it wasn't doing any damage but was serving a good purpose!

After this fiery demolition, we leveled the open field between the ruins. The remains were shoved into the small cellar area and covered with dirt. Dorm built a large sledge covered with planks, and, with his truck, towed it around the field loaded with laughing and shouting boys who provided weight for the grading operation. It sounds a bit crazy, but it worked, and in one weekend we had made a field for games: football, softball, capture-the-flag, and less organized mayhem.

It wasn't the Rose Bowl, but it provided the setting for a lot of fun and character building.

A little of the latter rubbed off on me. I had always loved football, but generally did more hollering and running around than getting in the thick of the action. However, one day as our side kicked off, one of the big guys on the other team caught the ball and began a wild runback.

I suddenly realized I was the only person between this behemoth (so he seemed to me, a younger boy) and the goal line. I gritted my teeth, ran right at him, grabbed him around the knees, and brought him down. I felt sore for several days, but the cheers of others made it worthwhile. After that incident, Dorm banned tackle football and required the less lethal "touch" variety.

Probably a good idea, since none of us had any sort of protective pads or helmet, and our field had a gravelly dirt, not grass, surface!

The Original Off-Road Vehicle

Getting a bunch of boys out to Tahuya and back to Bremerton posed logistical problems, especially when supplies and camping gear had to brought out, too. During the lodge construction period, both of Dorm's trucks (a big flatbed and smaller pickup) were required frequently, and occasionally one of the older boys came out in his own car.

This led to a problem one Sunday afternoon when it was time to say good-bye to the camp and head for home. We began to load the two trucks, and discovered a problem....a big problem. Dorm was there to drive the flatbed, but the fellow who had driven the pickup to the camp had gone back to town a bit earlier in the car of another older boy. There was no one left to drive the smaller truck.

Dorm looked around, scratched his head, and suddenly said, "Jimmy, you'll have to drive the small truck." I couldn't believe what I was hearing!

Jimmy....that was me! I didn't have a license, I didn't have a learner's permit (I don't recall that there was such a thing then), and, worse, I had never driven any vehicle "solo" before. Sure, I'd made the truck jerk along a bit under my dad's close supervision, but to drive it by myself—what a nasty thought!

There really wasn't much choice, so soon I found myself behind the steering wheel with a couple of brave (read that "foolhardy") kids riding behind. No one sat beside me in the passenger seat; they wouldn't be able to open the door and jump out fast enough in an emergency!

It wasn't hard to get the engine running. The truck was technologically advanced enough to have a self-starter. But automatic transmission? Only a few big cars, certainly no pickup trucks, had an early version of such a contraption. No, this truck had a stiff, unforgiving clutch. When I tried to ease out that clutch and tickle the gas pedal as I'd been told, Whoa! The thing leaped and bucked . . . . and died.

On the third try, we were on our way in low gear, bouncing and jerking down the rough dirt track. Eventually, we hit a paved road and I was able to shift up a notch. I began to feel pretty good rolling along at about 30 mph; only a lurking fear of what might happen when we got to town marred an increasingly satisfied feeling. I was driving!

Reality hit soon enough. As I looked down the road, I realized with a start we were coming to a T-intersection with a more important road, one that warranted a stop sign. I slowed down and managed to down-shift, but I was desperately eager to avoid coming to a full stop and having to get the thing underway again with its balky clutch and touchy gas pedal.

"Aha!," I thought, "I'll approach the main road very slowly, in low gear, look carefully to the left, and, if no one's coming (there's almost no traffic out here anyway), I'll just make the right turn without coming to a stop. Then it'll be clear sailing, at least until the stop light on Callow Avenue."

Good plan, but hard to execute, I found. As I approached the highway, I did indeed slow down, and looked to the left....and looked....and looked some more.

I heard shouts from behind, "No! No! Go right, not straight ahead!"

In my desire to be absolutely sure no one was coming from the left, I had slowly driven right across the highway and I realized that I was going down the slight embankment on the far side. By this time, I was aware of what I had done and made the right turn - around a huge stump, through some underbrush, up the embankment, and, with a bounce, onto the highway's pavement!

I learned later that boys in our big truck ahead were looking back, monitoring my progress. They were shocked to see the pickup slowly move right across the highway, disappear from sight in the brush on the far side, and then slowly emerge like a surfacing submarine, and climb back up onto the roadway!

Everything was an anticlimax after that. I was able to negotiate the dreaded stop light in Bremerton and follow the big truck to our meeting place at Charleston Baptist Church. I was a bit disgusted to note my passengers kissing the ground as they eagerly bailed out of the pickup. "No sense of adventure," I thought.

An interesting note is that my dad never did attempt to teach me to drive after that Sunday afternoon. I went into the U.S. Army at age 18 where I was forced to learn. I have loved driving ever since!

Tippy

In those times, most boys did not have pets at home. Bremerton, though not a large city, was pretty urban after all, and all our boys lived right in town. Also, the Great Depression, although it hit our Navy Yard town less than other places, had its impact. Thus the special importance of Tippy in a time when pleasures had to be simple.

Tippy was a large, brown Collie with a wonderful, highly-animated shaggy tail. He lived in the rundown farm that was the camp's nearest neighbor, a mile or so from the lodge. Not only did Tippy have a special place in the hearts of all Troop 511 boys, I'm sure we brought joy to his life too. Early in the construction process of the lodge, Tippy showed up one day on the site, drawn no doubt by the noisy clamor of twenty or thirty boys—and that can be quite a clamor! From then on, he learned to recognize the sound of our truck coming in on the old county road which passed near the farmhouse. He was out at the road by the time we arrived and ran behind the truck until we pulled into camp. Then, there was a tumultuous greeting with boys jumping around the dog, patting and calling to him, and Tippy, in turn, barking and licking and generally cavorting in that special joy shown best by dogs with boys.

Yes, Tippy was beloved of us all, and there's no question the feeling was returned. However, there was a time when love wore thin—at least for one weekend! Members of my patrol at the time—the Beavers—were all sitting around our camp-site (called "The Hogwallow" by the other patrols) one pleas-ant day eating lunch. We heard barking, first in the distance, then getting closer.

"What the heck's going on?" I thought, and then Billy cried, "Oh, no! Look at that!"

At that moment a skunk burst into our camp from the trail, ran across it, and out the other side, with Tippy in full pursuit! It was the first (and, as I recall, the last) time we'd ever seen a skunk at Tahuya, but Tippy sure had found it! A quick sniff revealed no skunk odor in the piney air, and we breathed a sigh of relief that the skunk had been going too fast to put his defense mechanism in gear before he rocketed through our camp.

We rushed up to the big field to see the outcome of the chase (kids are gluttons for punishment!). Tippy was coming back toward the lodge from across the field, looking rather dejected. The reason became clear as a breeze, from his direction, wafted toward us. Our beloved dog had apparently won the battle but lost the war. He must have caught or cornered the white-striped carrier of evil smell, forcing the skunk to release a good dose of it. I think Tippy was well aware of what our reaction would be when he attempted to approach, but attempt he did.

All the boys began shouting, "Go away, Tippy!" and the good dog did just that. He spent the rest of the weekend in the middle of the field, looking sad, as his erstwhile friends gave him wide berth. Fortunately, by the time we returned next month, all trace of skunk odor was gone and Tippy was our pal once more!

The Electrifying Cougars

In the early days at Camp Tahuya, all patrol camps lay south of the river. The nicely wooded areas atop the north bank beckoned invitingly, however, and one day Dorm announced that we would build a bridge. In several weeks a fine log and plank span linked both banks. It was fifty or sixty feet long and five feet or so above normal water level. We had seen that the river rose dramatically after hard winter rainstorms, and the bridge was built to stand above these flood levels. It did just that, and survived, at least during the years of Troop 511 history at Camp Tahuya.

About this time, I became leader of the Cougar Patrol, and we staked out a new campsite north of the river. I had a pretty sharp group of boys, including Bob, a budding inventor/engineer. We built a little paddle wheel to power an automobile generator at what we called "Cougar Falls," a drop of about three feet along a branch of the river. The generator was to charge a battery, which, in turn, would provide power for two lights in our shelter at the patrol campsite.

One weekend, after several hours of hard work, the great moment arrived.

"Throw the switch!," Bob ordered.

I did . . . and nothing happened! Not even a flicker in the light bulbs!

We discovered that the paddle wheel was not of advanced technology, even for the time, and couldn't turn the generator fast enough to produce much current. Later in the evening, however, with members of other patrols watching, we threw the switch again and beamed proudly as the first electric lights at Tahuya shone on the Cougar camp!

All the other patrols and even the lodge had only lantern light!

We never did tell the others that it was the storage battery that was powering the lights and that the generating system was a flop. Sure, we had to sneak the battery back to town every now and then for a recharge—but what the heck, the Cougars still were the only ones to have electric lights!

Snipes and Other Indignities

Most of the kids in Troop 511 were of what currently is called the "right stuff." Even with our outstanding Scoutmaster and his assistant, the troop couldn't have accomplished what it did without good Scouts. Yes, there was horseplay and some roughhousing, but, overall, a great feeling of camaraderie and pulling together dominated. However, even the best group of boys can't resist teasing an easy mark. And 511 had a couple of those boys.

One was a good but obviously vulnerable kid named Murray.

Secretly, I think we all admired Murray for the way he took the teasing and the practical jokes pulled on him every now and then.

The first joke dealt with snipes. When I officially joined the troop, several of the troop veterans talked about taking me on a snipe hunt when we were out at Scout Lake. After some

buildup about what great eating roast snipe was, I was rarin'
to go. However, for some reason, it never happened, probably
because I had already been initiated with the great "midnight
hike for water" caper.

During Murray's first Saturday with the troop at Tahuya, someone suggested a snipe hunt for him. Murray being Murray,
everyone thought that was a great idea. By this time, I was in
on the gag and willingly went along with the customary buildup
about how easy it was to bag snipes, and how great they tasted
cooked over a campfire.

That night after dark, a gang of us set out with Murray. (Everyone knows that snipes can only be flushed out in pitch black-
ness!) We hiked down a dark, old logging road for a half mile
or so. Even though several of us had flashlights, it was pretty
creepy. The towering, black fir trees took on almost human-
like forms against a sky which was only slightly lighter.

Murray squeaked, "Do we have to go much farther?"

Johnny, one of the oldest kids and leader of the hunt, said in a
hushed, though kindly, voice, "I guess we've come far enough,
Murray. You know, the snipes won't roost close to the camp—
they don't like the noise people make. That's why we had to
come quite a ways."

How reasonable, how kind Johnny sounded! At his quiet call,
we all gathered in a small group—to tell the truth, it felt good
to be near others out there—and Murray received his instruc-
tions. He was given a gunny sack and flashlight and was told
to hold the bag open with the light shining out directly above
the opening. The rest of us would fan out in a circle around

him and begin stomping and beating the underbrush. This activity would rouse the snipes from their nests, and they would fly up and be drawn to the light, so Murray was told. All he had to do was to close the bag after several snipes had flown in; once in, they would be confused and wouldn't be able to find their way back out again. He was told to call us when he had several, and we'd all regroup and head triumphantly back for camp with the catch. Murray would be the camp hero for providing good eating for the next day! We never discussed how the snipes he was to catch were to be killed, cleaned, and cooked, and Murray had enough sense not to ask!

No one beating the brush, of course, could use a flashlight because it would draw the snipes away from Murray. We found ourselves doing the beating in small groups; not because we were afraid to be doing it alone in the dark—of course not!—but just because it happened to work out that way. Each of us knew that while there really were no snipes out there, we didn't know what else might be!

We made a lot of racket at first and then, by plan, got together and began to work our way back to camp, making less noise as we retreated. In all previous snipe hunts the "victim" hadn't taken long to realize he'd been had and to come back to camp spluttering with indignation. We got back, had a good laugh with the fellows who had stayed behind, and waited for Murray to come stumbling down the road. After all, he had a good light and nothing really could happen out there . . . could it?

The obvious answer became less obvious as time went on with no Murray in sight. A rescue party with good lights was dispatched and found no one near the spot where the "hunt" had begun. I had a reputation for having the loudest mouth—lit-

erally—in the troop, and I was pressed into service bellowing
"Murray" over and over. Our bugler sounded his horn to provide direction. It wasn't a particularly cold night, but the joke
was rapidly wearing thin and real concern was setting in, especially with Dorm and Bill who were ultimately responsible.

Just when we wondered if we should hop in the truck to get
outside help, we heard a faint voice calling, "hello, hello!"

We shouted back and, in a few moments, Murray appeared
across the field, coming from quite a different direction from
where we had set out. In a sense, Murray had the last laugh
because no one was making fun of him now; in fact, he was
greeted as somewhat of a hero—none of us would have wanted
to be out there in his shoes, lost in the dark in an unfamiliar
camp. Murray's initial reaction, incidentally, was one of cha-
grin that he hadn't bagged any snipes!

It would be nice to report that Murray was treated with dig-
nity and respect thereafter; nice, but that wouldn't be correct.
There was, after all, the case of the all-night talk-fest. I was
still a Beaver at the time, and the patrol had turned in at a
respectable hour and were lying around the campfire. However, my next door neighbor and best pal, Billy, Soupy (another neighbor kid), and I kept on talking for a long time.
Sometime after midnight, we got the idea that we were going
to stay awake all night. So, propped up on elbows, we chatted
on. The subject of conversation, although no doubt of cosmic
importance, has long faded from memory. We kept poking
sticks onto the fire to provide a bit of warmth and light as we
bravely kept up our all-night vigil. However, about 3 a.m., we
had run out of wood within reach and the fire had died. What
to do? It was too cold to get out of our warm bags and chop

more wood. Our eyes fell on Murray, sleeping blissfully next to us, and suddenly one of us—there's nothing to be gained by specifying who!—had a great idea.

We sneaked Murray's big pocket watch away from beside his folded jacket which was serving as his pillow, moved it ahead to 6:30 a.m., and returned it to its original position.

Then we poked Murray and said "Hey, Murray, time to get up and build a fire. Johnny (the Beaver Patrol leader at that time) said it was your turn today."

Poor Murray grunted and groaned and looked trustingly at his watch. Without a word, he pulled on pants and shirt in his sleeping bag and crawled out. In a few minutes, he had a good fire going. We then broke the truth to him . . . it was like April Fools Day in November. He said nothing; just crawled back in his bag and fell asleep almost instantly.

Yes, the extra shot of heat and light allowed us to finish out the night without sleeping. It was rather a hollow victory when you consider how miserable and strung-out we felt all day Sunday! What happened to Murray? He slept in until 9 a.m. and was raring to go all day. He never mentioned the incident, and neither did we. I always had a suspicion that he didn't even remember getting up, but he must have wondered why Billy, Soupy, and I were so droopy all day!

The Mighty Tahuya Conquered Again

Nineteen forty was a year of big bridge building in the Puget Sound area. Both the first Lake Washington Floating Bridge and the original (and ill-fated) Tacoma Narrows Bridge were completed with much fanfare. This greatly excited me, and I began to feel that one bridge between the banks of our river wasn't enough; think of the disaster if it failed and we north-bankers were cut off from the lodge and field!

So plans for a second bridge began to unfold, first in my head and later on pieces of paper. This was to be a grand suspension bridge—the Tahuya Narrows Bridge! The selected site was far from narrow, but it offered several trees that could help support suspension cables. Of course, there was no budget whatever for the bridge, but I wouldn't let that stop me. On one truck trip from Bremerton to the campsite, I spotted a long length of cable left from an earlier logging operation. Sure, it was a bit rusty but clearly more than adequate for our modest needs. We induced Dorm to haul it to camp, although he plainly thought our scheme was crazy—crazy, but at least harmless, was no doubt the way he viewed it.

In fact, Dorm, acting now more as father than Scoutmaster, helped in other ways. He allowed us to take scrap wood out to the camp for our project from Braman Millwork. It was mostly slats from boxes for shipping glass. Then he drove me, my younger brother Bob, and sometimes another Cougar-helper, to camp for several consecutive weekend work parties on the bridge. Of course, this meant two round trips: one Saturday morning and Sunday afternoon. I guess you could say that in a way my mother helped, too, by not raising an objection to my missing Sunday School several times. Regular attendance at church and/or Sunday School was a firm part of life in the Braman household.

I had been enjoying—yes, I said enjoying—algebra and geometry at school and, with the help of a handbook I picked up somewhere, had developed some idea of the stresses involved on the wires that connected the cables to the bridge deck. Of course, I had no idea of the strength of those wires and cables, but, somehow, the stresses didn't seem to be too large. After all, the cable was pretty thick even though a bit rusty from lying in the woods for twenty or thirty years! In any case, I gave the plans my stamp of approval and construction began at "Tahuya Narrows."

It wasn't easy, especially since I was working alone part of the time, but several weekends of work saw completion of the great span. The south end approach was probably twenty-five feet across a small pond. The span was constructed of poles from the woods and the glass-box slats, and had a pole railing. This span led to two tall cedar trees which provided the "towers" for the southern end of the first of two suspension spans of perhaps fifteen or twenty feet each. A tree in the middle, supplemented by a pole I erected, provided the central towers, and a similar tree, again supplemented by a pole, provided towers on the north bank. The hanging bridge deck was in sections of four or five feet, attached to the suspended cables, hanging by heavy wires from Dorm's mill in great arcs like the bridges I had seen in Tacoma and San Francisco. The bridge deck sections were connected by loops of the same wire.

I was alone on the Sunday afternoon that the project was completed. Of course, I had walked on portions of the bridge during construction, but made a personal ceremony of my first walk across the full length of the span. Walking out on the suspended portions, I noted with great satisfaction that it moved and swayed a bit like a good suspension bridge should, but, overall, it felt secure. I didn't know at that time that the noticeable movement and swaying of my example—the original Tacoma Narrows Bridge—was the cause of great consternation among structural engineers and that the bridge would undergo a spectacular collapse in a moderate windstorm six months after completion!

We held a formal opening during the next regular monthly troop camp-out at Tahuya. My brother Bob and I built a little booth where we passed out goodies for those joining us in the celebration. I made a sign forming an arch between two trees at the entrance pathway, proclaiming to the world that this was the "Tahuya Narrows Bridge." What pride I felt as other scouts began trooping across the bridge! It was somewhat of a bridge to nowhere, although a trail on the far side did eventually wind its way to the Cougar campsite. But somehow its mere presence there in the wilderness justified its existence.

My pride turned to horror later in the day when I returned to the bridge site. Coming up the trail I heard great shouting and—could it be!—laughter. I burst into a run and found about ten scouts on the middle of the span over the open river (which at most seasons was just a good-sized creek) jumping up and down in unison to see how much the bridge would swing and sway. As I attempted with some degree of success to cool the action, I felt my sense of fear that my beloved bridge was to have a one-day lifespan slowly being replaced with a glow of immodest pride. Tahuya Narrows was tough! It had taken all those miserable kids could dish out!

In retrospect, I have wondered how it did stand up under the abuse it received, but stand it did for at least the two additional years of scouting I enjoyed before heading off to the University and ultimately the U. S. Army. When, shortly after completion of "my" bridge, the shocking news of the collapse of the Tacoma Narrows Bridge passed through Bremerton where so many people had viewed and crossed the span with pride, I couldn't avoid thinking that at least one Narrows Bridge was still standing in Washington State!

One time, not long ago, I drove back to the site of old Camp Tahuya. The lodge had been demolished; squatters had broken in from time to time and lived in it in the 1970s, and it had clearly become an unsafe nuisance. Looking toward the field that had been so laboriously leveled with Dorm's sledge, I saw that several houses had been built as part of some sort of country-living development. As I turned back to the lodge site, suddenly the whole scene flashed back; the lodge was there, smoke curling from its chimney, the 48-starred Old Glory flying from the pole in front. I thought of the Tahuya Narrows Bridge and hurried up the still-visible path, past the site of the old Beaver Camp shelter now long gone, and on to the bridge site. At first, I saw nothing but the waters of Tahuya River gliding by—even they had shifted course somewhat in the intervening forty-odd years. Then I squished out to the big, twin cedar trees that formed the south tower and smiled as I noted a cable still attached to one of the trees and trailing under the river to the far side. Yes, the spirit of Tahuya Narrows lived on, and there was still some visible evidence that here once stood the realization of a boyhood dream.

Chapter 4

COUGARIA

I've always had a "thing" about imaginary cities and countries. Some of my earliest memories are of playing "city"
behind furniture as my mother vacuumed the rugs. Not many
people are as lucky as I and been able to enjoy careers built on
childhood dreams, but becoming a city planner seemed almost foreordained for me. I won't relate how the reality sometimes did not match the dream, but, overall, I retain my feeling of good fortune.

When a boy with such visions in his head suddenly finds himself in charge of a Boy Scout patrol, and all the while in the
background he is reading of Adolf Hitler's spreading conquests,
strange things can happen. The rise of Cougaria was one of
these.

Cougaria was mostly a mental and, overall, quite harmless
exercise. This imaginary country embraced the "territory" at
Camp Tahuya which the Cougar Patrol considered its own.
All of the other patrols, in the Cougar's eyes, were countries
too: Beaveria, Lionia, Eaglia, and Hawkonia. For some obscure reason, the Lions were the "enemies"; the Beavers or, as
we referred to them, Beaverians, were talked into becoming
allies. Lionia, headed by patrol leader Andy, was akin to Nazi
Germany, and Andy (a likeable, non-aggressive kid) was, in
our imagination, the Hitler-like dictator.

It's important to know that this was strictly a Camp Tahuya
phenomenon and was largely one-sided. Away from camp,
we were pals with the Lions as with all other patrols, and there

remained a strong loyalty to 511 and its boys. In fact, no one but the Cougars, until the climactic weekend, paid much attention to "Cougaria." Our troop leaders took little note of the whole phenomenon.

But we Cougarians fancied that Lionia threatened us. We tightened our alliance with the Beavers and began making defensive preparations. In the woods above the south bank of the stream, we threaded wire in the underbrush and made a couple of "forts" along the wire, which we grandly termed the "Herrigstad Line" (Herrigstad being one of the patrol members). The forts were figurative "caves" in the underbrush, well stocked with pine cones for lobbing at an attacking enemy with peepholes for spying on his troops.

We planned for some more high-tech measures too. One was a trip-wire system. Anyone breaking a segment of wire would activate a battery-powered electric warning signal indicating the direction of incursion. We planned to string the wire around the back of our camp—pardon me, country—to preclude a sneak attack from the rear. This great program never got off the drawing board. The long range artillery project did, however.

The artillery we referred to as "rockets" since several of us were devotees of science fiction magazines of the day. Our rockets were like long crossbows with segments of truck tire innertube as the propellants for our blunt cedar arrows. We designed these projectiles to carry chemical "stink bombs" into the enemy camp and thus demoralize his troops. On one of the Tahuya Narrows Bridge construction weekends, when only Cougaria's technical advisor and I were in camp, we carefully calibrated our weapon with field tests.

. . . . . . General Volchock of the Lion Empire Army sat in a bunker in Beaver City, which his ruthless forces had just over-run. He was sharing a victory toast with his officers when his orderly ran in with a warning,

"Sir! We have word that some sort of enemy projectile is streaking toward us!"

"Damn," muttered the Lion commander, "The reports that those dastardly Cougars have developed long range rockets must be true!"

He rushed to the viewing slit in time to see the projectile arch-ing down from the sky short of the city. It exploded with a muffled roar near the river shore where any harm would be minimal. In a moment, though, he saw another rocket scream-ing in; this would explode much closer to our headquarters, he thought. Clearly they were getting the range! The next salvo might mean the end . . . .

These were my thoughts as I hid under the tables in first the Beaver Camp and later the Lion's, while scientist Bob would lob arrows into the camps. I would spot them coming in over the trees and report on where more or less force on the inner tube band was required for a relatively direct hit. After a couple of hours we had the proper positions of the inner tube bands marked for the two camps.

You may well ask why we zeroed in on our allies, the Bea-vers. It had to do with the overall strategy for the impending war. Our plan was to goad the Lions to attack. Since the Beaver camp was close to the Lions and on the same side of the river, the allied forces would fall back rapidly at first and let the Lions occupy the camp. Then the stink bomb barrage would begin!

In spite of Bob's general scientific expertise, at least relative to his age of 14, he never developed a transportable stink bomb with reliable trigger mechanism, so we never had the warhead we wanted. Even if we had, we knew within ourselves that we could never use it because the wooden arrows were potentially dangerous (in the unlikely event that our calibration really was accurate enough to guide a direct hit on the campsite!). But it was a lot of fun to think about and plan for these science fiction-type approaches.

Our plans for "war" were real enough, however. We convened an "international" parley to develop written rules of war. They came out remarkably like the old game of "Capture the Flag." When a person was on enemy territory, he could be captured by being hit on the back three times by a captor who would have to cry "caught, caught, caught!" when rendering the deadly blows. The prisoner would then be held in the defenders' "capital" and could not leave unless one of his own troops, without being "caught," was able to get in and touch him. If that happened, both opposing warriors could return to their own land without interference. The only weapons we could use were pine cones (most were from fir trees, but, for some reason, we always called them "pine" cones). Rocks, fists, and sticks were strictly taboo.

In looking back, I can see we weren't taking any chances on losing this war. First, we had an ally so it would be two patrols against one. Second, we had drawn the countries' boundaries in a way that favored our strategy. The other patrols thought we were pretty nutty, I suspect, but they willingly agreed to our battle plans.

We planned that the first monthly trip made after the signing of the rules of war would be the "big one." On the Saturday evening of that trip, the tension in the camp was so strong that everyone could feel it, or so we Cougarians thought! To goad them into a fighting mood, we taunted the Lionians, who seemed to ignore the whole matter up to this point. We had stored huge stockpiles of pine cones in our forts and at other strategic places. As I lay in my sleeping bag that night, sleep didn't come easily. My thoughts became mixed up with what I had been reading daily about the war in Europe. Did the Lions have surprises in store for us? Would our capital be hit by dive bombers the next day? Were our defensive plans adequate to forestall the feared Lionian blitzkrieg? As the Cougarian leader, if I were captured would I be subject to degradation or even torture in the feared Lion concentration camps? No, I thought firmly as I finally drifted away. Justice and right would triumph.

Sunday dawned hazy but dry . . . we were ready! Of course, war had to wait for practical things. Breakfast was first priority. And then Dorm always had a little church service for the boys. I don't remember his topic that morning, but I hope it wasn't "peace on earth" because immediately afterward we implemented our plan.

First, we stationed a small band of front-line forces in highly visible positions near the Beaver-Lion boundary, hurling insults at the Lionians. We wanted to maneuver the Lions into being the aggressors, and, sure enough, it didn't take long for them to attack.

"President Braman," Bob cried, "The Lions have crossed our border in force!"

"Retreat!" I responded.

This withdrawl was not as cowardly as it sounded; it was part of our strategic plan to lay a trap. The whole Lion Patrol (in our eyes, the entire Lion army) raced forward toward the Beaver capital. The din was awful, pine cones flew, and our outnumbered forward force began its planned if rather hasty withdrawal across one branch of the stream, where they were joined by other Beaver-Cougar troops. Here we made our stand.

As we expected, the enemy, with a cry of victory, stormed into the Beaver camp, Beaveria's capital, and splashed across the stream toward Cougaria to join in final conqest. But what's this? First, they were met with a dreadful hail of pine cones, and then suddenly they were being pinned down individually by defenders who pounded their backs and cried lustily, "Caught, caught, caught!"

They had taken the bait and unwittingly stumbled into Cougar territory because of the tricky way the map had been drawn in the rules of war. Most were captured in short order. Whether, under other circumstance, they would have submitted willingly to the rather outrageous rules will never be known because they were badly outnumbered and were in no position to defy their captors.

There were a few Lion soldiers remaining (not many, since a patrol only had eight boys, and we'd already captured most of them). One Lion made a brave but foolhardy attempt to break into our camp to set a captive free, but he ended up in our prisoner of war stockade. We, of course, abided by the Geneva Convention and treated our prisoners well. In fact, we plied them with goodies so they'd see how much better was the Cougarian way of life than what they endured under the wicked regime in Lionia! Shortly, our brave forces, bolstered by the knowledge that they numbered thirteen to the Lionian defenders' two, smashed into Lion City, the enemy capital, and ended the war with total victory.

What followed gave Andy, dictator of the evil Lion Empire, a bit of a pause. When time came to conclude what we called the Treaty of Mossyrock, named for a feature of the area at which the peace conference was held, he was surprised to be handed a typewritten treaty draft. He knew there was no typewriter for miles around and deduced that I had prepared this treaty in Bremerton before we ever left home for Tahuya.

He spluttered, "Braman, you knew there was going to be a war, and you knew just how it was going to come out!"

True, I thought, but immaterial.

With a what-difference-can-it-make sigh, he signed the humiliating document. I only remember one of its terms, but it was a doozy. Lionia had to cede all of its river waterfront to Cougaria, with the exception of a three-foot space adequate for them to come to the river to get water!

Of course, once the victory was ours, the Cougars quickly forgot the whole battle and other patrols forgot it even sooner— except for me; in the innermost recesses of my imagination, Cougaria and the other countries lived on! They provided the basis for maps of fictitious planned cities, names of teams in athletic leagues, schedules for railroad systems, and other trappings of countries with more physical substance than Cougaria. What a waste of time! What a misuse of creativity! What fun!

A postscript: Those treacherous Lions didn't abide by the terms of the Treaty of Mossyrock; I saw some of them brazenly get water outside the permissible 3-foot zone! I wonder where Andy is now? Is it too late to bring him before the United Nations for treaty violations committed more than five decades ago?

Top- Logging operation for lodge at Camp Tahuya
Bottom- Sundown Lodge under construction by Troop 511

Top- Sundown Lodge and "The Bus"
Bottom- Enjoying the fireplace in Sundown Lodge

Top- A Troop 511 "Gypsy Tour" caravan
Bottom- Changing one of several flat tires (Yellowstone trip)

Top- Time for bath...in icy mountain stream (Yellowstone trip)
Bottom- Dorm cooking dinner on the road (Yellowstone trip)

Top- Camp at Home Sweet Home, Olympic Mountains
Bottom- Winter camp at Flapjack Lakes, Olympic Mountains

103

Top- Huge Western Red Cedar tree at Lake Quinault
Bottom- Five new Eagle Scouts (Dorm Braman on left)

104

Chapter 5

THE WINTER CAMPS

The Flapjacks

During its heyday, Troop 511 was anything but in a rut. Although a monthly camping trip to Tahuya was the norm, there were exceptions. I've already mentioned the summer mountain hikes which took the place of Tahuya visits (more about them later). For three consecutive years, the troop made special midwinter weekend excursions. The first two involved backpacking, long before snow camping became popular (well, at least relatively common!).

For our first winter adventure we hiked to Flapjack Lakes in the Olympic Mountains. There's no doubt that Dorm was an adventurer at heart. None of us, including him, had ever been to Flapjack Lakes before. But we had good maps and information, and the trail was correctly reputed as easy to follow. Today the lakes lie about eight miles from the end of the road at Staircase camp and from the base of the fearsome Wagonwheel Lake trail mentioned earlier. Fortunately, the old road up the Skokomish River was open in those years so the distance to the lakes by trail was only a bit more than 4 miles. However, the elevation gain was more than 2,500 feet so the trail required a significant effort.

This adventure started on an early December Saturday morning. About 20 boys piled onto the covered back of Dorm's truck and into the cars of Bill Juneau and a father of one of the boys. In a little more than two hours we reached the trailhead above the winter-swollen Skokomish River. We slung on our packs and began at once to pound up the trail. We were spared the heavy winter rainfall that is a hallmark of low elevations of the Olympics even though it was a typically gray day. I was still quite young compared with many of the boys, but much strengthened since the earlier Wagonwheel Lake hike. Our leaders required that everyone carry his own sleeping bag and very limited personal needs. Boyhood pride just wouldn't have allowed anyone else to carry those things! But the older and stronger fellows carried most of the food and cooking stuff.

We hadn't yet had any truly cold weather that winter and didn't run into snow until well above the 3,000 foot elevation. I gave a silent prayer of thanks. It was hard enough to put one foot in front of the other time and time again without having to drag them through snow! We must have been a sight as we puffed up the trail, resembling a train with 20 locomotives, breath billowing from each of us like steam into the damp and chilly air. I'm sure I wasn't the only one who moved along in the trance that afflicts everyone after a certain distance of mountain hiking. The only difference was that some of us reached that state in about two blocks while others retained normal thinking and feeling a bit longer.

After about fifteen switchbacks in the trail and ten or so "blows"—brief pauses in hiking to sit or stand hunched over to relieve the strain of the pack straps on our shoulders—we reached a welcome site. Here stood the trail junction sign that proclaimed Smith Lake lay off to the left and Flapjack Lakes were just one-half mile to the right. True, it turned out to be a long half-mile, but, at that point, no one minded too much.

As we reached the shore of the larger Flapjack Lake, the pretty one with cliffs and the Sawtooth Range rising from its shore, we all flopped briefly on the snow. We had reached 4,000 feet, and there were about two feet of the white stuff on the ground in the open areas with less under the evergreen trees surrounding the lake. Although the clouds were low enough to prevent a summit view when we arrived, and I was truly tired, it was still a magical moment. Snow clung to the trees, and the pristine, white blanket around us was unsullied by any footprints. Except for our subdued puffing, we heard no hint of sound. Off to the left, the Bremerton Mountain Club's A-frame cabin, nestled in the woods under its snowy roof, made a Christmas-card picture.

Boys recover at a remarkable rate, and the snow only remained untrampled for about five minutes. Then snowballs flew and Tenderfeet and Eagle Scouts alike thrashed around in the snow. We never had snow like that in Bremerton, and most winters went by with none at all. Now, Dorm did his best to bring some order to the scene. He soon succeeded to the extent that we loaded our gear into the cabin, which we had permission to use for the weekend.

We only had about 24 hours to spend at the lakes, and part of the time we devoted to the business of keeping body and soul together. We spent much time cutting wood to keep the fire going in the cabin, an essential activity if we were to have at least one haven of warmth in the wintry scene. High quality winter gear hadn't been developed at that time, and we couldn't have afforded it if it had been. We wore a hodgepodge of heavy jackets, coats, wool caps, heavy boots all greased up with Hubbard's and whatever was available at home. As evening set in—this trip happened very early in December— the cabin was full not only of boys but also of a variety of wet

109

clothes and footgear hanging from the rafters and lying on chairs and the floor.

Dorm put a huge kettle of beans to simmer on the old pot bellied stove shortly after we arrived, and, just when the hunger pangs reached the intolerable level, big bowls of chili were ready. It was fiery, as Dorm always made it, but went down just fine with cups of icy water from melted snow.

Soon we were slipping into the sleeping bags that covered almost every square inch of the floor. There were no requests for stories that night; the strenuous climb and play in the snow had put even this energetic gang in the mood for sleep. As I lay there for a moment or two before slipping off, I sensed that hiking to this mountain lake in the winter snow was an adventure that would remain bright in a lifetime of memories. Time has proven this to be so.

I was usually one of the first ones awake at camp; I still haven't mastered the art of sleeping in. That morning at Flapjack, however, no one got up early. I awoke in the silvery light of dawn, very late for me and, after a cold run to the outhouse, noticed that it was going to be a beautiful, clear day. I finished dressing and ventured out by the lakeshore. Transformed by the winter sun, the scene was an absolute fairyland. The trees to the right were hard to look at for the brilliant sparkle of sunwashed snow on their branches. Mt. Lincoln in full height, rose above the far shore of the lake. The snow on the ground, although chopped up by yesterday's play near the cabin and lakefront, sparkled. My breath came out in large clouds, but the lack of any breeze made the cold quite acceptable. Soon I was joined by others, and we began breakfast preparations.

Immediately after eating, pal Billy, brother Bob, and I ventured out to do a little exploring on the neck of land that separated the larger lake at the foot of the mountains from the shallower, swampier one above the valley.

. . . . . . Captain Braman and his faithful guides Uumo and Nokki were grateful that the wicked storm of yesterday had ended. The Arctic blast had taken the lives of their sled dogs, and they had only the supplies on their backs. They knew their only chance of survival was to hole up until the relief team arrived. It was clear that the sunshine of the moment was but a brief respite and that the howling blizzard would soon engulf them again.

Uumo surveyed the land around, squinting into the low summer sun.

"Here, Captain." he said, "Here is the place for our igloo."

So, in the small hollow, the three went to work, packing snow into firm blocks which were arranged in a circle big enough to accommodate them. Then they laid more blocks in rows curving inward until one large block finally filled in the top. They had left a small hole on the leeward side and crawled into it.

"Good work, Uumo," said Captain Braman. "We'll be safe here for days if need be. Don't be concerned. The U.S. Navy won't let us down; my comrades will get here in plenty of time!" . . . . . .

The reality, of course, was far less dramatic; we never were out of sight of the snug cabin with its reassuring wisp of smoke. We had a wonderful time fashioning our crude igloo and, when climbing inside, felt like Arctic explorers. Other boys built two great snow forts with ample piles of snowballs, and a fine winter battle followed.

The troop planned to leave shortly after lunch to pound down the trail to the waiting vehicles, but an unforeseen event cut our stay a couple of hours short. Mack, while cutting firewood, took one mighty swing which went astray and cut through his boot and into his foot. Dorm and Bill, using the minimum first aid supplies we had, bound up the foot and stopped the bleeding. It was clear, however, that Mack would be doing no walking that day. The older fellows built a stretcher out of two poles and a couple of blankets. We all took off down the trail in a rather sober mood, hurrying as much as possible while still handling the stretcher safely.

Mack was in pretty good spirits, and we felt we could kid him about banging himself up to get a free ride down. Everyone took turns with the stretcher, and, even with that extra burden, going down was easier than coming up! Of course, we'd also eaten up the food, lightening the older fellows' loads.

The story had the usual 511 happy ending. Everyone got home in good spirits, Mack included, and he suffered no long-term ill effects from the rather nasty wound. It's interesting to recall that this was the only significant accident I can remember on the many hikes Troop 511 made over the next several years.

The Trail That Sank

The next year, for an early winter camp, we hiked into Lake Lena, also in the Olympics. We left Bremerton in Dorm's truck on an early December Friday evening. December is in the heart of Puget Sound's dark and wet season, and it was dark and starting to rain when we unloaded at the trailhead on the Hamma Hamma River. We planned to hike to our destination at Camp Cleland about two and a half miles up the trail. This camp was operated by Tacoma Scouts on the lake. We shouldered our packs and headed up the trail in darkness, alleviated only slightly by the carbide miners' lamps several fellows had mounted on their rain hats.

Slogging along a muddy trail that had a fairly steep upward grade, in the dark of night, and in rain which by now was heavy, might not be everyone's cup of tea. For teenage boys in a troop like 511, it was quite an adventure. After thirty minutes or so, the bright talk that characterized the beginning of a hike tapered off into a one-foot-in-front-of- the-other experience. In relative silence, we reached the shore of Lake Lena in a couple of hours and found the camp at the far end of the lake. Each of our patrols was assigned a cabin. These had shake roofs, wooden floors, partial walls, and wooden bunks for our sleeping bags. Being largely open, they were damp and clammy, but at least we were out of the rain.

Building a fire at the end of our cabin was a challenge since the fire pit was out in the open beyond the end of the roof. With the help of some dry paper and a lot of blowing by willing mouths, a blaze was soon crackling at the Beaver cabin. We saw through the gloom that other patrols also had their fires going. Perhaps the sight of blazing fires in the dark,

113

rainy night affected us because fire raids were soon underway, with boys carrying flaming brands through the wet night
and hurling them in the general direction of the other cabins.
The flaming torches made a lot of very satisfying hisses and
spark showers. It was really quite a fine pyrotechnics show.
Dorm soon got wind of what was happening and, on general
principle, put his foot down, and also, I can see in retrospect,
out of concern that someone might get burned. There was
certainly no danger to property; everything was thoroughly
soggy and even Smokey the Bear, if he had been born by that
time, could hardly have complained of forest fire danger!

We finally settled down in our bags and drifted off, listening
to rain pattering—no, thundering—onto the roof. Cooking
breakfast the next morning was a great challenge. We finally
got a fire of sorts going in the soggy fire pit, but cooking pancakes in a frying pan with heavy rain beating into it really
wasn't successful. I can't recall what everyone else in the
patrol did, but I remember drinking some of the maple syrup
and spreading jam on a piece of newspaper and enjoying Lake
Lena "toast."

Rain or not, we were camping at a lake, and, naturally, in those
circumstances, we felt we should enjoy the "beach." No one
was quite crazy enough to go swimming, but we did a lot of
rock-throwing and splashing around along the shore. We made
a pastime of pushing sticks into the sand at water's edge and
measuring the rise of the lake. And rise it did! Rainfall fell
steadily on the lake, and, no doubt, it fell heavier on the mountains above. We looked across the dappled water and saw
huge foaming streams cascading down the steep slopes into
Lake Lena. An enormous landslide had formed the lake centuries before. A visible scar extended nearly to the top of the

114

mountain across the lake. The rocky material that dammed the Lena Creek Valley and formed the lake was porous. During drier times, the outlet stream trickled through rocks below the surface of the slide. That was the condition we found when we had arrived the night before, but we all wondered what was happening when we noted how rapidly the lake surface was rising. Within an hour of their placement, the first sticks stood five or six feet out in the water along the shallow-sloping beach. From time to time, we added new markers and could see before dark that the lake had gained several feet in depth.

Because the rain continued all night some of us were ready to commence building a modern-day ark. By the time we packed up on Sunday morning to return to the road, Lake Lena had filled up to the high water level evidenced from previous flood stages. Our spirits were high, though, because we were headed to Bremerton where our homes had walls all the way up, roofs that didn't leak, kitchen stoves under cover, and furnaces that kept the chill and damp away.

We started down the trail alongside the lake comfortable in the knowledge that it was downhill this time and broad daylight, although a bit murky. This descent would be a snap compared with our Friday night slog up to Camp Cleland! We rounded a bend in the trail, scarcely 500 feet from camp, when the line of boys came to a stop.

Pete, up near the head of the line, said, "What the heck . . . . ."

Johnny, too, was nonplussed. "Geez, the trail's slid down the bank. What the heck do we do now?" he said.

Peering ahead, I saw the problem: the trail led neatly down a slope . . . and right into the lake! The water had risen about ten feet and the trail was now open only to underwater travel. This spot on the trail was low because it skirted beneath a rocky cliff. Dorm and Bill led us back a few feet, and we saw a rough path heading straight up the steep rocky slope. Evidently this wasn't the first time campers had had to escape Lake Lena by climbing over Chapel Rock!

With our packs, climbing the rock was a tough scramble. We inched upward, using underbrush to provide handholds, as mud and pebbles dislodged by those above rained down on hikers behind. This was long before the days of Gortex or even nylon. Those Scouts wearing poor rain gear were soaked by water from the sky and the bushes; those with rubberized, waterproof gear were soaked by perspiration from within. We had to climb about two hundred feet in elevation (or so it seemed at the time) and then make a more hazardous but a little less arduous descent down a similarly steep rocky and brushy incline on the far side of Chapel Rock. Never did a trail look better than the muddy track we joined at the base of the rock! When we reached the lake's outlet, less than two days from when we hiked in, the scene had changed dramatically. A raging torrent overtopped the old slide and plunged down the steep stream bed toward the Hamma Hamma.

Winter camp number two ended without further incident. Late on Sunday we pulled into the troop hall in Charleston where the boys were met by parents and taken home for good meals at real tables in dry homes.

I said to myself, "I'll never take these things for granted again!"

Rain, Rain, Go Away

The third winter camp began in late February the following winter at Lake Quinault, out near the coast, the wettest area in the then 48 states. The Grays Harbor Scout Council had given us the O.K. to use the facilities at their camp on the north shore of this beautiful, but rain-girt, lake. By this time, the troop had acquired an old Fageol bus (you'll hear more about that famous—or infamous?—bus later). So some of us traveled to Lake Quinault in the relative comfort of the bus; others went in the truck. It was a considerable trip: more than one hundred miles each way.

Not much urban development lay between Bremerton and Lake Quinault, mostly forested countryside with communities smaller than Bremerton such as Shelton, Elma, and Montesano. However, we did pass through the sizable twin towns of Aberdeen and Hoquiam, lumbering and paper-making centers on a Pacific Ocean inlet of Grays Harbor.

Before stopping for an interesting tour of the big paper mill in Hoquiam, we plodded through Saturday morning traffic in Aberdeen. This town was bigger than Bremerton. We were impressed with buildings up to eight stories in height, and there were lots more traffic signals than we had at home.

Such a signal brought my best friend Billy to grief. He had observed on other trips that Bud, a likable fellow a couple of years older than we were, with a great sense of humor and perfect timing, had a habit of leaning out the bus window when we passed by a good-looking, teenage girl.

He'd look straight at her with wide eyes and say in a drawl,

"My, but yore the purtiest gal I ever saw!"

This always brought a blush of pleasure and confusion to the target as we passed on by.

As we slowly moved down a busy street in downtown Aberdeen, a girl ahead on the sidewalk caught Bill's fancy, and, as we approached her, he leaned out the window and, mimicking the older Bud as best he could, said, "Gee, you're the prettiest girl I ever saw!"

He just got out the last word when the light ahead turned red, and Dorm stopped the bus. Bill was eyeball to eyeball with the girl on the sidewalk, and she stared him down . . . we then saw she probably was two or three years older than Bill! In this case, the blush and confusion belonged not to the girl but to Bill. Bill (and I, for that matter) never tried that trick again; we left such risky flirtations to Bud, the wily old master.

Upon arriving at the lake, we found fully enclosed patrol cabins at the camp, more adapted to winter camping than the shelters at Lake Lena. The weather, although a bit warmer because of the lower elevation, was just as wet; it rained all weekend. In this case, though, our senior leaders prepared all meals in the big mess hall, and we were cozy and dry. That is, we could have been cozy and dry if we wished, but spread out before us was a perfectly good lake, a really big one this time. In no time, most of the boys were out in large open boats, in groups for safety purposes, but acting as if it were mid-summer.

Water jousting became a favorite sport. A patrol would climb into a boat, with all boys manning the oars except for one especially brave soul who, with an oar extended, stood in the bow. He attempted to knock his counterpart from another patrol into the refreshingly cool (!!) lake water. Of course, there was a concession to the season; people dumped in were fully clothed and not just wearing a swimming suit! Only two or three boys actually ended in the drink, and they were quickly pulled out and rushed to the warmth of cabins. However, they weren't the only ones who got wet. These naval battles on the lake involved a great deal of splashing of oars. Some fellows rapidly became proficient in sending a large volume of water into an opposing boat with one good splat from the broad side of an oar.

Common sense eventually prevailed, and, after everyone had returned to cabins and dried off, the troop drove over to the other side of the lake and took a short hike on the Mount Colonel Bob Trail. That took enough steam out of us so that we rather quietly enjoyed our big bowls of split pea soup for dinner and the traditional story-telling and song-singing prior to turning in.

On Sunday afternoon our old Fageol bus, roaring along at its full level-road speed of 40 miles per hour (we made a little more than that going downhill and a whole lot less going up!) got us to Bremerton before dark. Families once again heard stories of a strange and wonderful weekend, but they didn't hear about everything. Even teenagers have enough sense not to tell their parents about water fights on Lake Quinault during a Pacific Northwest February!

119

Chapter 6

THE MOUNTAIN HIKES

1937 . . . Up and Away!

"Jimmy, it's time we joined the big leagues. Last summer, 501 and 504 took week-long hikes in the Olympics. By golly, no one's going to leave 511 in the dust!"

It was midwinter in Bremerton, and Dorm was poring over a map in our new home at Sixth and Highland. I knew that if those other troops had gone twenty miles he'd have us do thirty . . . at least! Still, the thought was exciting. Challenging the wilderness for a week! Climbing straight up perilous cliffs; hanging spread-eagled on steep glaciers; facing down bears; eating only what we could find or carry on our backs! The last thought was a bit daunting, considering how I liked to put away the grub.

"Yeah, let's show 'em what a real troop can do!" I said with bravado not justified by experience.

The first step was selecting a route for the 1937 summer adventure. Bill Juneau joined Dorm in contacting the Forest Service and also the National Park Service. Some of the route might cut through part of Mt. Olympus National Monument, predecessor to the later and larger Olympic National Park. Finally, they selected a route involving some challenge but still suitable for boys ranging from 12 to 17 in age.

In our downstairs meeting hall at Charleston Baptist, during a regular Thursday evening meeting, the troop heard the news.

"Gang, you know we've talked about a big mountain hike. It's not talk anymore; we're going to do it!"

Dorm's words were greeted with enthusiasm. "My experience over the years tells me that in our area, the last week in July and the first in August give us the best chance for sunshine and least danger of rain. That's why we'll leave on the last Saturday in July, the 28th, and come back to civilization on Sunday of the next week."

About 15 years later, Seattle's new Seafair celebration confirmed Dorm's amateur weather analysis. After an exhaustive study of long-term weather bureau records, officials chose those very two weeks of summer for the famous Seafair event.

"Here's the route we'll follow," Dorm continued. "We'll drive up the Dose ("Dosey," the nickname everyone applied to the Dosewallips River) to the end of the road at Jumpoff Falls, and then pack up the main Dose trail to the Forks where we'll hit the West Fork trail."

Dorm continued to outline a route up the trail to Camp Siberia near Anderson Pass, then over Lacrosse Pass and First Divide, and finally down the Skokomish River to the road's end. The total hiking distance with packs would be about 26 miles with several additional miles added for excursions from base camps. We'd be out for eight nights and would climb about 7,000 feet over the three passes (not counting the inevitable ups-and-downs of any mountain trail). It would be a challenge, but everyone was eager to go. Any misgivings would come later, when it was too late to turn back!

It's well to reflect a bit on the camping and hiking environment of the 1930s. Present-day equipment just wasn't available. As mentioned before, there were no nylon or Gortex materials, no light-weight hiking boots or packs. Sleeping bags were either filled with down (much too expensive for us!) or kapok. Kapok was heavier than down, and more of it was required to provide an acceptable level of insulation. Freeze-dried food had not yet been developed, and even staples such as powdered milk could not be found in grocery stores. Bremerton did not have a true sporting goods store. Even the equipment and products that were available were usually beyond the financial reach of boys in this Depression era.

Those were the negatives, but there was a "plus," and it was a big one. Few people hiked in the mountains in those days. Most of those who did hike were dedicated to the outdoors and cared well for the wilderness. No one could even imagine a day when reservations would be required to backpack in some remote areas, or a time when wood fires for cooking could not be permitted. A permit was required, however, to hike National Park trails (largely for purposes of safety and as a means to distribute fire-prevention information). But the whole process was pretty simple, and anyone making the effort would find a true solitary, wilderness experience when away from the few access roads that led into the mountains of the Northwest.

Under the circumstances, Dorm and Bill did a marvelous job with logistics. They researched the hiking magazines available at the time, went to bakeries, and located other sources, either locally or by mail order, for powdered milk, powdered eggs, canned butter, canned meat, powdered applesauce and apple butter, dried pea soup, and other lightweight foodstuffs that didn't require refrigeration. For that first hike in 1937, they also found a source for "pilot bread," a thick, round, un-salted cracker that could help fill up hungry boys without add-ing too much weight to their packs (although quite a lot of bulk). These crackers, along with cheese, raisins, and solid chocolate (all available in local stores even in those ancient days!) made up the "trail lunch" that we ate every day in the mountains.

Finally, after weeks of preparation by our leaders and of an-ticipation by the boys, the night arrived—the night before an early morning departure on the big truck and in several cars. What a scene at the troop hall that night!

Dorm had divided the common goods (food, axes, cooking gear) into piles of varying weights, ranging from very little for the youngest boys up to 30 pounds or so for the oldest. Each boy added the individual goods that he needed: his sleeping bag, bare minimum of clothing and personal gear, and, of course, the backpack. Most of the Scouts carried "Trapper Nelson" packs, made with a bent hardwood frame and can-vas—pretty fine stuff for that period and the standard for years to come. An interesting side note: during the development of this type of pack, my mother and Dorm helped the inventor. They cut the hardwood slats and, using a wash boiler at home, bent the slats to conform to a human back.

Reality began to sink in as boy after boy hefted his loaded pack. As one of the younger kids, my load probably weighed only 20 or 25 pounds. Even on the level floor of the hall it felt like someone was tugging at my shoulders in a football game. Of course, the younger boys didn't dare complain. Regard-less of our innermost thoughts, a show of nonchalance was necessary.

"Nuthin' to it, Dorm."

"Is that all the stuff you're going to give me?"

"Hey, watch my smoke!" and similar comments were heard.

Not so with the big kids—Johnny, Pete, Dan, Bud, and the likes. Their packs were a lot heavier, true, but they didn't need to put on a show. In fact, they flipped to the opposite extreme: "Who put the rocks in my pack?" "If you think I'm going to haul this thing up the mountains, you're crazy!" or just, "Oh, my achin' back"—a favorite saying of the times.

Regardless of our comments, there could be no doubt we were excited. Our first long hike, and it was going to be great!

The next morning, Saturday, a number of dads who had volunteered for the job showed up with their sons and cars and took on extra kids for the two hour drive to the trailhead. Some of the boys and their packs rode the big truck—that was a prime spot because there could be more horsing around on the big flatbed, thoroughly surrounded by safety fence! No one had even dreamed of seat belts then!

It was one of those special Puget Sound summer mornings— sunny and crystal clear. We drove along Hood Canal, a long inlet at the eastern base of the Olympic Range that everyone just called "The Canal." We turned up the gravel road along the Dose. As the cars and truck slowly ground up the long switchback above Elkhorn Camp, we knew that we were about to test our mettle as hikers. At midmorning, the vehicles came to the end of the passable road, and we all piled out, got our packs, and "saddled up." There were brave goodbyes for those boys whose dads had driven cars (and for the man from Braman Millwork who had come to drive the truck back to town). Then we turned our eyes westward up the trail.

Dorm had not been a member of the then-fledgling Boy Scouts in his youth; in fact, he had little hiking experience before his leadership of Troop 511. Yet he and Bill had good leadership instincts and did an excellent job in assuring safe, enjoyable experiences for their charges. From the outset, the troop followed a system of trail discipline that worked well. Dorm headed the line, followed by the youngest kids; this allowed him to gauge how they were doing and set the pace and rest stops accordingly. At the very back, several of the oldest boys and Bill Juneau trudged along at a pace slower than they probably would have liked. We younger ones always enjoyed calling them the "Poop-out patrol" because they tended to lag behind, intentionally, I'm sure, so they could enjoy their own camaraderie. No individual boy was allowed to lag behind or to go ahead. If Dorm sensed that someone desperately needed a rest, he stopped everyone to make minimum embarrassment for the flagging one.

But back to Jumpoff Falls on the Dose that fine July morning. An unfinished roadbed cut from huge cliffs flanking the falls actually formed the beginning of the trail. In just a few minutes, we were beyond this and into the real trail. We moved forward on the almost level trail at a slow, steady pace. The sound of roaring water from the adjacent river, the feel of the trail underfoot, the sight of moss hanging from the alders and maples, the sunbeams slanting down through the tall evergreens . . . it took but a few minutes for us to be caught up in the magic of the mountains. I get the same feeling on a mountain trail to this day!

The initial gently sloping trail was easy going and allowed us greenhorns to adjust with minimum pain to our packs and the discipline of step-by-step progress. After one brief "blow" for a bit of rest, we arrived at Dose Forks where we saw our first forest shelter. These open-fronted log-and-shake structures were found at many trailside camps in the Olympics at that period. Some had wooden slat bunks and could accommodate six to eight people for sleeping and also provide a sheltered place for cooking and eating in those rainy mountains.

We left the main river at this point and pushed on up the West Fork, crossing it on a log bridge high above a rocky chasm. As we plodded along the forested mountainside, we could barely hear the stream far below. We began to learn just how long a mile can be for a beast of burden without benefit of wheels or internal combustion engine. Still, it was with a strangely satisfying feeling of fatigue—and gratitude—that we finally reached our first overnight stop at Diamond Meadows, some six miles and more than 1,000 feet in elevation from our starting point.

Usually, Dorm, wisely, did not permit us to remove our packs during rest stops; he had us either stand and lean forward with hands on knees, or, for more serious rest, sit against logs and rocks with the weight of our packs removed from our shoulders. Not having to re-shoulder the packs made it much easier to get going again. Thus, at Diamond Meadows, we first experienced the sensation—the glorious sensation—of removing our packs while standing. The first few steps after pack removal gave us a feeling of walking with half-gravity, of virtually floating. We always looked forward to this sensation at the end of a hiking day.

Immediately, Dorm and his senior group built a fire at the front of the shelter. We never cut living wood for fires—in those days there was plenty of downed wood and dead limbs handy to the camp. I don't recall specific meals, but I remember that everything—with a couple of exceptions you'll be hearing about—tasted great. We consumed a few fresh things during the first couple of days. After that, we ate stews made from canned beef and vegetables, beans, rice and meat, beans, thick soups, beans . . . it didn't take long to figure out that Dorm loved beans, and, of course, they were easy to carry in dried form!

We all sat near the big campfire by the shelter. I had a hard time keeping my eyes from the dazzling night sky. I'd never seen so many stars! We were talking quietly; the magic of the moment precluded even the desire to hear one of Dorm's famed stories.

Suddenly someone said, "What's that?," pointing down the trail.

I could see a faint light winking through the trees and then the sound of someone walking along the trail.

There came a "Hallo!" from the direction of the light, and then a figure staggering under the largest pack imaginable came into the circle of light from our fire.

Dorm said, "Hi, Fred. I was getting a little worried about you."

Everyone jumped up to greet Fred, one of the older fellows whose job at his father's small grocery store across from our troop hall forced him to make a late start.

I thought, "Wow, that's pretty brave! Six miles on a strange trail, the last part in deep-wood darkness with just a bit of light from his carbide lamp."

With a smile, Fred unhitched his pack and sighed gratefully as he sat down. We all watched as he reached into the outside pocket of the Trapper Nelson and pulled out a big Hershey bar and peeled off the familiar brown paper and foil wrappings. Sure, we'd had a good dinner, and the applesauce for dessert had tasted fine at the time, but, oh, the look and smell of that chocolate! He slowly savored it, bit by bit, seemingly unaware of our drooling stares.

When he finished, Fred stood up, stretched, and opened up his pack. The reason for its unseemly bulk quickly became apparent. He pulled out several big boxes of candy bars of the era. In addition to Hershey's, there were Baby Ruths, Butterfingers, Looks, and Dam Bars.

He said, "Brought a few things up from dad's store. Thought candy might go pretty good up here."

Then, ever the entrepreneur, he set up shop! The bars were 10 cents each (they were three for a dime back at his store), and he would take IOUs!

It was a good lesson for us about supply-and-demand and also about the rewards of hard work. He sold every one of those bars that night, and our thoughts were not of profiteering but of gratitude! Besides, we knew instinctively that he had worked hard for his pay-off, carrying ten pounds of extra weight in candy over those six miles! Anyway, there was something about his carrying it in a pack for that distance that improved the candy's flavor. Never since has a Baby Ruth tasted like it did that night!

Early the next morning, after an oatmeal breakfast, we pushed on to Camp Siberia, our first base camp, which was below Anderson Pass. The way to Honeymoon Meadows—named for a couple of Seattle newlyweds who had spent time there years earlier—was steeper than the previous day's trail, and it got worse. Also, we frequently left the shelter of the evergreen forest and hiked out in the open under a hot summer sun. The "blows" became more frequent and were just as welcome as the past night's candy.

Finally, we arrived at the forest shelter at Camp Siberia—officially called Anderson Pass shelter—for a three night stay. The weather belied the popular name of the camp—it was sunny and warm during our entire stay. The time spent at this camp made it clear why men (surely we qualified for that title after our struggle to get there) loved the mountains. We found a lovely stream at the base of a huge shale slope. It was topped by sheer cliffs etched against a deep blue sky. Dorm's rule that no one could wander off by himself, that a "buddy" system must be followed without exception, was observed by everyone.

This restriction didn't deter some exciting wanderings, however. A group explored to the top of the shale slope—known by mountaineers as a scree. It was a tough climb, starting in large boulders that had tumbled from the cliffs high above over the centuries. It led up to the slippery shale on which two steps forward literally resulted in slipping one step back. There was an unforeseen reward, however. The intrepid fellows, arriving at the base of the cliff high up the slope, noted a little hole several feet higher. It could only be reached by one boy standing on the shoulders of another—a precarious operation at that height while standing on shale—but one that resulted in a marvelous discovery. The hole was filled with clumps of quartz crystals!

Soon the word was out, and the slope resembled pictures of Chilkoot Pass during the Klondike gold rush, with a line of boys clambering up and others sliding down. Before long, just about everyone had a cluster of crystals. The best specimens would have perhaps eight or ten large, clear quartz crystals, up to four inches in length, sprouting from a rock base. Other samples featured smaller, slightly yellowed crystals, but each boy saw his find as a special treasure. I'm certain everyone who was there still has memories of what we dubbed the "Crystal Mine" at Camp Siberia. It didn't dawn on us until later that these crystals were HEAVY. We still had about 18 miles to go to the end of the road on the Skokomish River, with two mountain passes to cross to reach our goal! But I don't recall that anyone abandoned his precious crystals along the way.

Mack's Lost . . . or Not

Our troop devoted one of our days at the Camp Siberia base to a short walk up to Anderson Pass. We gazed into the fabled Enchanted Valley of the Quinault River with its precipitous walls and many waterfalls, and then struggled straight up a

131

three quarter-mile stretch to the base of Anderson Glacier. This elevation afforded a first-time, close-up view for many of us of a living mountain glacier. This broad stream of ice was probably a mile and a half long—it has greatly receded since that time—and was broken by many crevasses showing the blue ice of the glacier's interior.

Dorm let us walk only on the very edge of the glacier, recognizing the dangers inherent in both the visible crevasses and those that might be hidden under a snow crust. Still, being on that sheet of snow and ice made us feel like explorers. The rocky soil right alongside the shrinking glacier was reputed to be a good place to find loose quartz crystals, and we had some success in a hunt for them. However, the discovery of the crystal mine with its much larger treasures took the edge off this. As fog began to roll in across the glacier, we ate our trail lunch of pilot bread, cheese, raisins, and chocolate, washed down with Koolaide chilled with chucks of glacial ice chipped off with pocket knives. The food may have been a bit primitive—though none of us complained—but no restaurant ever had such a view!

Finally, fog rolled in to blanket the area to the point of little visibility, and Dorm thought it best to return to camp. We lined up and counted off, our usual practice on this kind of side trip, and came up one short! A repetition brought the same result. After a moment or two of checking, we found that Mack was the missing one. Dorm immediately knew that there were two possibilities: Mack had wandered off and was lost in the fog somewhere, or, contrary to orders, he had returned to camp earlier on his own.

While some of us hollered into the fog for Mack, Dorm was

132

busy thinking.

Something clicked, and he called out, "Boys, gather 'round. We've got to find out right away if Mack went back to camp. If he didn't, we have to get Juneau and the older fellows that stayed in camp up here to help us search."

Dorm had thought of a fast way to do this. He stayed at the glacier and sent one older kid off at the head of the whole group. This group went downhill as fast as they could safely go. Another older kid brought up the end of the string of boys. At about every 250 feet, he would tell the boy just in front of him to stay at that spot. In just a few minutes, a chain of Scouts extended from Anderson Glacier to Camp Siberia where the lead boy found Mack talking with the others . . . bless him; he had returned on his own! Immediately the word went up the chain, "Mack's in camp!"

Thus in ten or twelve minutes Mack's whereabouts was known, and the need for a harrowing and pointless search avoided. Needless to say, upon his return, Dorm gave Mack a little speech about obeying the rules!

The next day found us hiking over LaCrosse Pass to camp in the Duckabush Valley. No, that's not a misprint. The Native American names on the Olympic Peninsula, or, at least their English translations, are wonderful; they include such other names as Humptulips, Hamma Hamma, Soleduck, and, as you've heard, Dosewallips.

My principal memory of this long drag in the sun is that I kept talking all the way. It seemed to help me ignore my misery, although, from the comments of others, it increased theirs! I also learned an unexpected fact about mountain hiking; going downhill was no piece of cake either! The continual braking action to maintain traction and control on the rough surface, multiplied by the weight of the backpack, was tough on the front leg muscles. By the time we had dropped 3,000 feet from the summit to the valley camp, there were many pairs of very wobbly knees in our group. Removal of the packs at the end of the day, however, brought about quick relief.

At the end of this day, one big fellow we nicknamed Bowcutt, a sturdy hiker, was more tired than usual. He had complained since lunch time about his pack getting heavier with every mile. Of course, most of us felt this way so we paid no attention. However, when he flopped down at the Duckabush camp and opened his pack, we heard a bellow of outrage. He found several good-sized rocks in his pack . . . and not just the crystals everyone was carrying. Plain, dirty old rocks! At every blow, someone had sneaked a rock into his pack. How this got started I don't know, but an admonition from Dorm that it wasn't funny was enough to prevent a recurrence. All of us thought that Bowcutt was pretty tough to have survived the day as well as he did.

The Jello That Didn't

The following day, we climbed again to Home Sweet Home camp—an aptly named spot on a beautiful flower meadow with a lofty, snow-crowned mountain across the valley and a waterfall tumbling down the cliff at the back of the camp. One incident makes the Home Sweet Home sojourn especially memorable to me.

I always enjoyed playing in, or dreaming by, the creeks that almost invariably flowed by our camps. We camped by these steams to get drinking and washing water, the former being the much more important to teenage boys! It was always assumed the streams in the Olympics were pure and suitable for drinking, and we used them this way without thought. In fact, we scoffed at the one or two boys who had moved from the East when they asked if the water was safe to drink! No one had ever heard of giardia at that time, and, indeed, I wonder if this affliction is some sort of latter-day invention. The fact is that I recall no illness striking down anyone on our hikes in the Olympics, and we sure drank from plenty of trail-side streams! Bear in mind, that, at that time, only a few humans were using those trails.

One morning I was playing on the stream that tumbled over the waterfall behind the shelter. I noticed that a dry watercourse came down the steep, rocky slope only six or eight feet away from the rushing stream. The news was full of great river-related projects those days: dams, irrigation systems, flood control, and the like. Of course, the troop had already seen the greatest of these--Grand Coulee Dam.

As I sat by the stream, I hatched a marvelous scheme: the mighty river (as it had become in my always-active imagination) would be diverted! So I went to work moving rocks and scratching at the rocky soil with sticks to build a channel between the stream and the dry streambed. When this was done, I used rocks, leaves, and debris to dam the main stream so that its flow was diverted into the new channel. Finally, success! My hard work was rewarded by the sight of a new stream, flowing in the channel I had created and down the formerly dry parallel channel, with the water coming back into the old streambed 100 feet below.

Yes, the Braman Diversion worked . . . worked too well, I discovered at dinner time. Our dessert was to be fruit gelatin, a favorite of mine. In the morning, after boiling water in a large kettle and adding the fruity powder, Dorm covered the hot kettle, put a rock on the lid, and placed it in the icy stream to set. And it would have set, except, at the spot he selected, the stream shortly thereafter went completely dry, a victim of the great waterworks project! I wasn't too popular with either Dorm or the boys as we drank lukewarm gelatin heated by the hot sun that beat down on it all day. As I now realize, the fatal flaw in my project was failure to prepare an Environmental Impact Statement so that all ramifications of the diversion could be fully understood before it was undertaken.

Some Like It Hot

Our first great hike was nearing an end as we climbed the relatively short elevation to First Divide and dropped down into the Skokomish River valley. We joined the river at Nine Stream—there were so many side streams joining the Skokomish along the valley that early explorers adopted the expedient of numbering them! The last several miles were easy—on a soft-tread trail in deep forest beside the lovely river. At first glance, our last stop at Camp Pleasant seemed to live up to its name. However, the swarms of gnats that arose from the dry moss on all the surrounding trees made life pretty tough.

These gnats didn't spoil our appetites, however, and Dorm cooked the last dinner on the trip: split pea soup from the mix he had obtained by mail order from California. It was a little thick, the open fire a bit too hot, and the result was predictable—the soup scorched. Dorm tested it, made a face, and,

136

recognizing that there wasn't anything else to cook and no store just down the trail, fixed the problem in the only way he could think of. He poured in pepper, then some more pepper. A smile crossed his face as he tested it again. Dorm loved hot food . . . he could virtually drink Tabasco sauce as an appetizer!

He told us it was great, and we lined up for hearty bowls. We sat down to eat, and, as a body, we rose and rushed to the bank of the river. There twenty-five famished Boy Scouts ate scorched pea soup, made fiery by the concentration of black pepper. The routine was one bite of soup, one gulp of water. It was rather rough going, but the alternative, starvation, was most unappealing, so eat we did. I must note that this was the only meal during the nine days that came out, shall we say, a bit short of perfection.

The next day found us in great spirits hiking down the last few easy miles to the trail head and waiting dads with truck and cars. Even a flat tire on the truck during the homeward trip along Lake Cushman and Hood Canal couldn't dampen our enthusiasm. Part of this elation came from knowing that we had done it; we had conquered three mountain passes in the Olympic wilderness! And, by golly, we did it pretty much with flying colors! But even then, if challenged, I would have had to admit that some of the enthusiasm came from knowing that night there would be fresh meat for dinner, a visit to the Ice Creamery, and, later, a soft bed and pillow to end the day!

1938 . . . "I Can Beat the Sun!"

"Wow! Look at the elevation gain! More than 5,000 feet."

"Yeh. And it looks like a lot of switchbacks."

Dorm and Bill were poring over a quadrangle map of the Elwah River area in the northern Olympics.

"I only hope your old Chevy truck can make it."

"What the heck," Dorm concluded, "We can make it up there somehow. At least it will be nice to start a hike high and go downhill when our packs are heaviest!"

With these comments, our two leaders determined the route for our 1938 mountain hike. We were to drive up to Port Angeles, then to the nearby Elwah River and up the notorious Hurricane Ridge road to Obstruction Point. This wasn't the beautiful Hurricane Ridge highway that today is negotiated from Port Angeles by anything on four wheels (or even two wheels!). No, indeed, this was a narrow dirt road that reached the ridge via many switchbacks up 5,000 feet from the Elwah River. From Hurricane Ridge, we'd continue driving on a narrow road to Obstruction Point, ending at an elevation of about 5,500 feet. (The Obstruction Point road hasn't changed much in 50 years and still affords an exciting, scenic drive.) Here we'd hoist packs and set out on a hike of about 25 miles. Quite a bit of the distance would be cross-country or on faint way trails in some of the most glorious mountain scenery imaginable. However, the great views would be hard won, as we were to discover.

We made similar preparations to the previous year, except for a few changes to capitalize on lessons we had learned the first year. Dorm hadn't been too fond of the pilot bread so he came up with an original idea: he talked a local bakery into thoroughly toasting hamburger buns just short of melba toast. A taste test showed that they were light, crispy, and tasty. Boxes of them wouldn't weigh much, but they would be a bit bulky in packs. Dorm used this fact to good psychological advantage. He gave younger boys boxes of the toasted buns as their share of food to carry. The boxes made impressive looking, but not heavy, packs—good for the self esteem of Tenderfeet!

When the day of departure arrived, it was warm and sunny, and the old truck was packed with boys and their gear. The trip to the base of the Hurricane Ridge road was uneventful, but excitement ran high as the truck began grinding its way up the steep dirt road. With each steep switchback turn, the scenery improved. Through the fir, hemlock, and spruce trees we began to catch glimpses of the high, snow-crowned peaks of the Bailey Range. The air smelled fresher, the sky was bluer, and our spirits higher as we crawled upward. As we turned yet another corner, the truck sputtered to a halt. Dorm climbed out of the cab and said, "Well, fellows, looks like I goofed. I should have filled 'er up at that old gas pump down on the Elwah. Judging from the gauge, we won't have enough juice to get to the top and back down again."

So he did the only thing possible: he unloaded all of us, turned the truck around on the switchback, and headed back down. It seemed like a long wait, but, in an hour or so, we could hear the truck motor grinding its way up the grade . . . at about ten miles an hour! We had another emergency stop as we approached the summit when the truck began to overheat, its radiator needing more water. Luckily, there was some moisture trickling down the bank, and, by digging a little hole and scooping out water by the cupful, we got the radiator filled to a safe level.

The road was steep and narrow all the way up, on a mountainside which plunged down to the river below. This wasn't too worrisome as long as we were in trees, but as they thinned out and timberline approached, the view down was more frightening. Finally, we were traversing open meadows on what we termed an "Orphan Annie" road, one carved out of the steep bank with an open drop below, a phenomenon common to the old comic strip of that name. At one point where the road had partly washed out, Dorm stopped and got out again. We could hear the distant roar of the Elwah 5,000 feet below and were looking straight out at the glaciers of Mt. Carrie across the valley. However, as we unloaded the truck at Dorm's command, our attention was focused on the road ahead. The relatively long washout had reduced the width of the road to little more than the distance between the tires on the left and right sides of the truck! Since we still had 9 or 10 miles to the end of the road, we couldn't stop here!

Dorm said as nonchalantly as he could, "It looks O.K., gang, but we won't take any chances. I'll drive 'er across alone, and you guys can walk along behind."

The man saying this was not only our Scoutmaster, he was also my dad, and I was not enthusiastic about this approach. Still, there didn't seem to be much choice if we were to have a hike that summer. Perhaps he did think it was O.K., but I noted that he drove across very slowly in the lowest gear, and had the driver's door open with his left foot on the running board, ready to jump out if necessary! As he moved onto the narrow area, our eyes focused on the downhill side. There was about six inches between the tire and the nearly sheer dropoff of the washed-out area. Miniature avalanches of dirt

140

trickled down, loosened by the vibration of the truck wheels. We trudged along, trying to look unconcerned. I probably wasn't the only one doing a little praying at the time!

Dorm reached the relatively wider roadbed in a minute or so, though it seemed a whole lot longer. We cheered, hopped back aboard, and gave this close call no further thought as we ground on to the trailhead. Come to think of it, I'm sure the employee in my dad's firm who came along to drive the truck back to Bremerton gave this situation a little more thought, especially since on the return trip he'd be driving on the downhill side of the truck!

This Valley is Grand

We had a non-typical beginning to our hike. For a mile or so, the trail was almost level, out in the open with grand scenery. And then it plunged down and down into the Grand Valley. This experience of starting high and hiking down was unusual and great, although our feelings were tempered a bit by the fact that we'd have to climb out of the valley later. Still, since we would end up nine days later at a much lower elevation than we started, we had more downhill than uphill on the hike, and this was a cheering thought.

Eventually, we passed the first large lake in the valley where the trail resumed a modest uphill grade. We stopped at the second lake to make camp. A sign proclaimed this to be Lake Gladys and so we called it, although I have noted on more recent maps it is labeled Moose Lake. The latter name is a bit silly because moose are not among the many animals found in the Olympics. Regardless of its name, it was a delightful place.

141

Where the Fuzzy Marmots Grow

After our first dinner on the trail, cooked in big pots over a campfire, I walked a bit away from the cluster of tents and sleeping bags spread out on the ground and sat on a rock in the early evening light. The water of the little lake was absolutely calm, mirroring the steep, gray, cliffs on the opposite side. Beyond the cliff, peeked the top of a higher mountain with small snowfields burnished to gold by the setting sun. I barely took note of the happy buzz of activity in the camp, but my ears perked up as I heard a shrill whistle from up the valley. A marmot! And where there's one there's always more, and soon the evening air was filled with the whistles of marmots. In my imagination, I visualized mama and papa marmots calling their little ones in for dinner. Whatever was really going on, the mountain valley filled with a wonderful evening songfest as the whistles sounded and echoed from all directions. Soon darkness fell and a chill crept in so I returned to the campfire for a round of human singing, less melodious, perhaps, but no less cheerful than the marmot concert.

Later that night, the evening chill turned downright cold, and my rather thin sleeping bag really was no match for the night air. I shivered a lot and fancied I was awake all night. Indeed, I was awake when the first morning sun hit the high peak across the lake, and I watched the progress of the sunlight—painfully slow, it seemed—as it came down the cliff. When it finally reached the spot where I was lying, the warming was immediate and I jumped up and got dressed. I discovered it wasn't my imagination; it really had been cold that night. One of the boys had a little pup tent, with an icicle hanging down from the peak a foot or so above his head almost to his nose. During the night his breath had condensed and frozen! We had some fun kidding him about the gruesome death he could

142

have suffered if the icicle had broken off and plunged into his throat . . . killed by an icicle he had unknowingly created himself!

Fortunately, that was the only really cold night of the hike, and milder nights, combined with my getting acclimated, resulted in no more midnight shivers. And the two ensuing days we spent at Gladys (Moose?) Lake were happily spent in exploring, eating, climbing, eating, story-swapping, eating . . . you get the picture.

Tuesday morning, was bright and sunny again—time to hoist packs and say goodbye to our lakeside home. Heading up Grand Valley, we soon left the main trail and followed a faint path past a tiny mountain tarn and into a basin forming the headwaters of Grand Creek. The wildflowers were beautiful and the marmots greeted our coming with a chorus of whistles which echoed off the steep hillsides around us. The turmoil in Europe and Asia seemed very, very far away that glorious morning!

Our Own Icefield

It was a short and easy climb to the pass—really just a ridge top—which separated Grand Valley from the deep basin of the Lillian River beyond. We stood briefly, admiring the peaks on the far side of the valley. Dorm pointed out Mt. McCartney and the glistening ice of Lillian Glacier, our destination for the day. It didn't seem far away and most of us thought "piece of cake!" What we didn't know was that the faint path we had been following petered out at this point, and we had to beat the brush across steep slopes to reach the campsite. Even though undergrowth at this high elevation was less dense than

143

along the river bottoms, it was still tough going. Dorm and Bill consulted their topographic map frequently, and we were able to progress steadily if slowly.

At one point, we emerged into the open and faced a traverse across the base of a rocky cliff with an extremely steep slope below.

I said to my pal Billy, "I don't like the looks of this one!"

Though he said nothing it was clear from the look in his eyes that he agreed wholeheartedly. Dorm and three or four of the oldest boys moved gingerly across the steep spot, moving sideways, facing into the cliff base. Then Dorm came back and led the rest of us one by one across the hazard with a his left arm gently holding our right elbows as we inched across. The passage proved not to be so difficult as it looked, but I believe every boy there breathed an inward sigh of relief to be across.

It was easier going after that. We stopped by a little creek for our typical trail lunch. The Ry-Krisp, cheese, raisins, and chocolate were all washed down by Koolaide made from the waters of the icy stream. Then it was a short push on to a rocky plateau beneath the snout of the glacier. A challenge here was for each boy to find a little grassy spot for his sleeping bag amid the boulders left by the retreating glacier. Back then, none of us had ever heard of air mattresses. The absence of rocks in the middle of the back and the bonus of a little grass or spongy moss to act as a skimpy mattress was the minimum requirement for a decent night's sleep.

Here we were truly in the heart of the mountain range. In the three days we spent there, we saw not another soul; even the marmots didn't seem to get this far! But in this glorious spot we felt that our Creator was especially close. He was surely looking after us, because, even with Dorm's strictly enforced precautions about going nowhere alone, there was still a great deal of exploring around rocky clefts and foaming waterfalls by groups of two or three buddies. Our only casualties were occasional scrapes and bruises from minor tumbles.

After one fine dinner of beans and canned meat, topped off by toast with apple butter cooked from a dried mix, we sat looking down Lillian Valley and up at the mountainside beyond. The sun had just gone behind Mt. McCartney at our backs, and we were in shadow, but the scene before us still shone brightly.

Suddenly Buck, probably overcome by the euphoria of the moment, blurted out, "I can beat the sun!"

"What the heck do you mean?" was the response to this claim.

"I can get to the top of that mountain across the valley before the sun sets on its top!"

"What? I'll bet you can't!" came a chorus of voices.

The challenge was too great. Buck, an older boy and capable of taking care of himself, although apparently a bit daft at the moment, set off with Dorm's acquiescence, his progress tracked by our leader's binoculars. Dorm exacted a promise that Buck would turn back the minute he knew he couldn't make it, or no later than when the shadow had actually climbed to the peak.

Even those of us who had "bet" against Buck secretly admired him and almost hoped he could do it. Dorm and Bill knew better, that there wasn't a chance, even though the peak was, by Olympic standards, an easy climb, really just a very tough walk. The knowledge that Buck wouldn't face a long hike back down in the long twilight was no doubt why permission had been given. Our leaders were right. By the time Buck had crossed the river the shadow was already one-third the way up the slope. He had climbed only a short way up the steep slope when the sunlight winked off the top of the peak, and a look through the field glasses showed that Buck had turned back. The taunting he received on return was minor, and even tempered with some comments of "Nice try anyway, Buck!" We all respected a guy who would even attempt such a "mission impossible."

On Friday morning, we bid a most reluctant farewell to our glacier campsite. Few, if any of us, would ever be here again, but we would never forget it. For some, sweating it out three or four years later as soldiers, sailors, or fliers during "the War," memories of this idyllic corner of the world would help get them through tough times.

The first part of the day's hike involved climbing up the glacier, a new experience for all of us. We climbed on snow at the upper fringe of the modest icefield. Dorm led the way, tramping footsteps in the snow, and, with our hob-nailed boots and careful walking, there was little danger of sliding down into ominous-looking crevasses at the lower reaches of the glacier. Little danger, that is, except for Murray. Poor Murray had only regular shoes, not the required hiking boots. This had somehow escaped Dorm's notice before we left Bremerton, but, up until now, his shoes had only resulted in extra blisters

146

and discomfort. Here his slick soles posed a potential hazard, and Bill Juneau walked close by him as we slowly plodded the half mile to the ridge above the glacier.

Once on the ridge it was a fairly easy scramble around and over large boulders to the summit of Mt. McCartney. It wasn't Everest, but, sitting atop the 6,784 foot summit, the highest in this part of the Olympics, gave us a thrill. And the view couldn't have been much better with Lillian Glacier at our feet, the deep valley of Lost River to the west, and the much larger, blue-ice glaciers of Mt. Olympus, highest in the range, glistening against an azure sky backdrop.

Bud Comes Through

The topo map showed a way trail—these were just faint trails, not maintained in any regular fashion—below us, way below us! We scrambled back down to the divide above Lillian Glacier, and then inched our way down the steep slope to the trail hundreds of feet below. At one point we slid down a steep slot one by one, digging our heels in the loose dirt and holding on to bushes to keep the descent under some degree of control. Billy was the last one down, and for good reason. The noisy descent of 40 boys had aroused a family of bees, and they were giving him a bad time. I don't recall that he was stung, but he sure wasn't taking any chances by barreling through at high speed!

Although the trail wasn't much, just a path through sloping meadows marked by rock cairns, it brought the end of our cross-country hiking and allowed us to pep up the pace. We stopped for another trail lunch, this time near a small lingering snowbank, which allowed us a special treat, "slush-aide."

We mixed extra-strong Koolaide with snow in this concoction, an early day version of a Slurpee, long before 7-11 Stores were even dreamed of. After lunch, we pushed on, with Bill Juneau's "poop-out" patrol of older boys deliberately lagging behind. At one point, Dorm sensed that the main group of boys was ready for a blow, so we stopped and sat down by trail side, all pretty thoroughly beat. Just then we noted that Bud, a key member of the "poop-outs" and always the joker, was slowly creeping toward the forward group. As he passed boy after boy, he was sagging lower and lower, until finally he was crawling with pack on back, the picture of abject exhaustion.

He crept close to Dorm, looked up piteously, and said in a breaking voice (but one loud enough for all to hear!) "Dorrrm, what are we stopping here for?" That caused a great laugh and broke any sense of fatigue in the rest of us. We were now ready to push on. Bud was a character, but he was good for morale!

The final part of the day saw us re-entering timber and hiking down a series of switchbacks on a well-developed trail to Dose Meadows, a small opening along the north fork of our old acquaintance, the Dosewallips River. We had been in great country, had done a lot of tough cross-country hiking, and were feeling good. We'd be home in two days with fine stories to tell the folks there. Dinner was especially welcome that night and, finally, even the glutton patrol, a select group that finished up the leftovers after everyone else was satisfied (I was de-facto leader of that patrol), sat down contentedly. We had enjoyed chocolate pudding for dessert, a special treat made with powdered milk and pudding mix . . . and a real trick to cook over an open fire without scorching. From his little log

148

cabin at Dose Meadows, the forest ranger joined us as we sang around the campfire. The stars were especially beautiful as we bedded down on the relative softness of meadow grass. It didn't take long for sleep to arrive, helped along by the sweet murmur of the nearby stream.

The north fork trail the next day, an Olympic Mountain main stem, seemed like a super-highway compared with what we had been hiking over. We traveled more than 11 miles over this broad tread, losing 2,650 feet in elevation in the descent to familiar Dose Forks camp. The Dose was always within earshot, and often within sight, making for a pleasant hike. Several times we had human company in the form of other hikers going upstream.

Our well-ordered group, with Dorm at the lead and Bill taking care of the rear, must have looked pretty sharp to the several people we met. But not so another group of Boy Scouts. We passed this troop, that shall go unnamed, coming up the trail. First came the Scoutmaster, whom Dorm greeted warmly, followed by a small group of boys. Then others straggled along the trail with poorly-organized packs for a distance of perhaps a quarter of a mile. Finally, more than a half mile behind his nearest compatriot, struggled a lone Tenderfoot. No adult or older boy brought up the rear. He asked us meekly if he was on the right trail and was his troop up ahead? We reassured him about this, but felt both a sense of disgust with this mob— we didn't want to dignify it with the term "Boy Scout troop"— and pride at being members of Troop 511, a real gungho outfit!

We camped that night at Dose Forks; where our North Fork trail joined the one going up the West Fork. The previous year, we had passed through that camp at the beginning of our hike. Thus, our overnight stay might have been nostalgic, but that's an emotion not experienced much by teen-age boys! We weren't emotionless though. We felt the usual last night excitement about getting back to home, families, and other friends the next day.

"Coming out," as we referred to the end of a major hike, was always a big experience, and the 1938 event was especially fine. The weather was superb, our morale high, and a great feast awaited us at road's end. Many parents had come to meet us, and they had brought splendid picnic lunches. Those who couldn't come up also sent along food. We had piles of fried chicken, sliced ham, potato salad, fruit and vegetable salads, cakes and cookies, milk and soda pop . . . with all the seconds and extras anyone could want. The only thing missing was my favorite—ice cream—and for that treat I knew I only had to wait until the evening.

It didn't take long after our return to begin wondering what would be on the agenda next summer; where would our nine-day hike take us? We didn't know the fates (and Dorm!) had something quite different in store for us for 1939!

Chapter 7

THE GREAT TRIP OF 1939

Ready, Set . . . .

I don't know exactly when the greatest adventure of Troop 511 was conceived. Neither do I know whether it resulted from acquiring our bus, or whether we acquired the bus to accomplish the adventure. I do know that early in 1939 Dorm and Bill located an old 1920-something Fageol bus. They thought that this vintage vehicle would be just the thing for transporting the boys of 511 to Camp Tahuya and maybe farther afield.

The Bus. We never gave it a pet name; we just called it The Bus. But that implied no lack of affection. We had a lot of fun in The Bus and at the places it took us. I'm sure that the affection felt by Dorm and by the mechanically-minded dad who helped him was tempered by exasperation as they toiled to keep this old monster running. Finding parts meant a search of junkyards all over Puget Sound; even tires were hard to come by. But keep it running they did, and the Fageol never seriously—well, not too seriously—let us down.

No doubt it was under-powered even by 1939 standards. It had about six gear speeds, and getting up even a modest slope meant much downshifting. On the way to Camp Tahuya, older fellows would sometimes get out and walk alongside The Bus as it ground up a 7 percent slope. Just a normal brisk walk was enough to keep pace.

But having The Bus, our own 511 Special, was unique in the

153

annals of Kitsap County scouting and in itself was a source of pride. When Dorm informed us that The Bus was going to take us to Yellowstone and Glacier National Parks that summer, excitement began to simmer and then rose to a full boil as the time approached.

A number of things had to be accomplished before the big trip, and they occupied the energy of boys and dads alike. Work parties were needed to ready The Bus. In addition to preparing the engine and drive train for the 2,500 mile trip, we built storage boxes to go on top of The Bus and under some seats. We fitted jump seats in the aisles so we could take 36 boys. Someone painted a fine sign on each side of The Bus reading "Troop 511, Bremerton, Washington . . . Home of the Pacific Fleet."

Then there was the matter of money. Dorm aimed to keep the per-boy cost low enough so that everyone who wanted to go could do so. He hoped to have a little left over to quietly subsidize several Scouts who might not be able to afford any payment. The Lions Club had already paid for the site of Camp Tahuya and The Bus (it cost $200 as I recall!), and we could not reasonably expect them to come up with more. So we embarked on fund raising of our own.

A huge paper drive became our principal source of income. Bremerton had never seen the likes of this effort before. My Cougar Patrol provided an example of participation that you'll read about later.

In the end, we hauled enormous truckloads of paper to the purchaser in Seattle. The price for used paper to be recycled was good (though we hadn't heard the term "recyle" then).

154

The old papers netted many dollars for our fund. Boys also took on odd jobs of their own to raise cash. In the end, we had raised enough money so that we could set the cost of the 15-day trip at just $10 per boy. This included all costs of running the bus, necessary camping fees, all food, and a little for emergencies—a provision which later proved to be wise! We planned to prepare all our own meals on the way, keeping food costs to the minimum.

The third preparation Dorm assigned to me. I contacted various places along our route to determine where such a large group could camp, preferably without charge. Dorm had told me the general areas where we should plan to stay each night, based on the daily mileage capabilities of The Bus. Dorm's plan gave me guidelines for my contacts. I wrote to state governments for information about state parks, to local chambers of commerce, and to national forests and parks. It was exciting to watch the mail each day for responses. Eventually, I lined up, with Dorm's approval, a list of probable spots for bedding down along the way.

The night before departure, all of us met at the troop hall for a final briefing. Then we packed our personal stuff, food staples, cooking gear, and other paraphernalia into the big storage boxes and under tarps on the roof-top luggage carrier. We lined up proudly alongside The Bus as cameras clicked. The *Bremerton Daily News Searchlight,* our local paper, ran a feature story about our departure. We were ready!

The Sproutmaster Saga

The next morning The Bus was parked at the service station owned by Mack's dad. It made a good assembly point—just six blocks from the terminal of the ferry that would take us to Seattle as the first leg of the 2,500 mile trip. I'm not sure anyone in the troop had ever taken a trip this long; I know that I hadn't!

Soon every one was there . . . except Mack! It was getting close to the time we had to roll in order to catch the ferry. Catch that ferry we must, because the old bus would never be able to make up time for any delay involved in waiting for the next boat to Seattle.

Just when we thought we might have to leave without Mack, someone shouted, "Here he comes!" Sure enough, after a squeal of brakes, Mack's dad, full of apologies, discharged a somewhat frantic Mack.

In seconds we were rolling down Pacific Street and onto the ferry dock. Then came the first of many obstacles that had to be overcome en route: as we moved down the ferry slip, we found that at the present level of tide, the load atop The Bus was too high to clear the roof of the car deck. The emergency required a bit of quick repacking. Fortunately, the ferry couldn't leave while we were half off and half on. In moments all was well, and, in the sunshine of a bright July morning, the ferry steamed off for Seattle with 36 exuberant boys aboard.

The first day went well enough, and our spirits were high as we rolled toward our destination—Sacajawea State Park near Pasco, a distance of 250 miles from Bremerton. We enjoyed our first lunch on the road, one that would be repeated nearly every day. Dorm pulled The Bus off the highway at an appropriate spot, set up the folding wooden table he had built, and, with the help of a couple of older boys, made peanut butter sandwiches from several loaves of bread and huge jars of the pasty stuff that kids (and most adults!) like so well. Along with Koolaide and cookies, and usually some kind of fruit eaten out of hand, we enjoyed our lunch. Yes, it sounds monotonous, but I recall nothing but pleasure each time noon rolled around.

In late afternoon we drove by the little farming village of Richland, not dreaming that in three years this sleepy town of less than 250 people would be transformed into a city of more than 20,000. It would bcome one of two principal sites for manufacture of components for the world's first atomic bombs.

Near Richland our first mishap occurred. We heard a muffled "bang" and then a slight thumping sound. Dorm recognized immediately the blowout of one of our four rear tires. We had strapped two spares on top of The Bus, and it didn't take long to jack up the old Fageol and replace the ruined tire with a new one—well, not new but at least fully inflated and in fairly good condition.

We arrived at the state park late in the day and admired green lawns and trees in this otherwise arid area. Vistas of the confluence of the mighty Columbia and Snake Rivers, as well as the name "Sacajawea," stirred recollections of the Lewis and Clark expedition that had camped at this very spot. The two rivers still flowed freely here since only Rock Island, Bonneville, and Grand Coulee Dams had been completed along the Columbia; later construction of more dams in postwar years would convert most of the Columbia and Snake Rivers into reservoirs. However, the Snake River at this point was placid, and Dorm told the boys it would be O.K. to wade in the stream

157

to clean up and cool off. Most of us did so, in shorts or underwear because we certainly wouldn't be caught dead in swimming trunks! We felt darn good at the end of the first day of the big adventure. Tomorrow most of us were going to experience a "first" in our young lives: going into another state, Oregon.

We cooked dinner in the big park shelter. Reverend Pyle of the Charleston Baptist Church, who had volunteered to fill in as assistant when Bill Juneau was unable to take two weeks from his job at the Navy Yard, helped Dorm with the cooking. We had the luxury of park tables for eating dinner, then enjoyed going back in the river and generally horsing around until darkness fell. We turned in early, lying on the lawn in our sleeping bags.

By mountain hike standards, the turf provided soft beds, and we would have drifted off quickly except for an unforeseen but significant circumstance. It was Saturday night at the only large park in the vicinity of the nearby towns!

Right after dark, cars began to roll into the parking lot. We had previously shared our space with no one. At first the cars just sat there, lights off, silence within.

"I think that kids are coming out here to neck," said my pal Bill, lying in the bag next to mine.

I quickly realized that he was probably right, although neither of us knew much about such nocturnal activities. Still, it wouldn't have bothered us, but the crash of a bottle breaking on the pavement was a clue that other activities were afoot. Soon the noise level became greater, and it was apparent that a beer party was under way, no doubt a part of the Saturday night double bill at Sacajawea State Park.

Soon a bottle-bearing female discovered the groups of boys lying in the dark and learned it was a Boy Scout troop. She bellowed, "Boy Sprouts! There are Boy Sprouts here! I'm gonna find myself a Sproutmaster!"

There was a lot of giggling from the dark shapes on the ground, but the good Reverend was shocked and stormed out to be sure that Dorm's sanctity was kept inviolate. In those less violent days his efforts were just met with laughter. Soon, however, our attention was diverted by potentially more dangerous activity. Two young men on motorcycles roared through the lawn area where we were lying. Because of darkness and their drunken state, they might easily have run over someone.

"Watch out," cried a voice from one of our boys.

"Let's show these crazy guys," cried another, "Get 'em!"

The 511 stalwarts were agile, leaping up in their underwear and easily avoiding the roaring behemoths. This "sport" didn't last long; one of our gang lobbed a sizable rock at a rider and scored a direct hit. With a curse he fell off his bike. Any thought of revenge on his part or that of his buddy who pulled up to lend a hand was stifled when they saw a large number of shapes in the background.

"You asked for it . . . ." and "Wanna make something of it?" several figures shouted.

Boys or not, some were pretty big and they badly outnum-

159

bered the biking duo. With more cursing the bikers rode away, not to return.

Dorm and the Reverend gathered up the boys and had them move their bags to a more remote spot. After a short period of whispering and muffled laughter, all was quiet until the dawn.

Slowly, Slowly Rolls The Bus

Our second day, rolling through the brown hills and green Wallowa Mountains of eastern Oregon, went well for most of the morning. Many of us got some exercise by trotting alongside The Bus as it ground up the mountain grades of U.S. 30. While in The Bus, we filled the time with chattering, dozing, singing songs, and horseplay, tinged with talk and speculation about the exciting events of the previous night. We teased Dorm some, asking him whether he had a good time with the woman looking for the "Sproutmaster."

As we motored at a pretty good clip through the rolling ranchland, the relative calm was broken by shouts from the rear of the bus, "Dorm! One of our wheels is passing us up!" "Hey, look at that, would you!"

And sure enough those on the right side of The Bus were treated to the strange sight of a tire rolling majestically alongside the slowing Bus and finally passing it. The tire leisurely veered into the sagebrush and disappeared. Since we had dual tires in the rear, The Bus stayed under control as it squealed to a halt.

The boys thought this was great fun. But Dorm, realizing his last spare would have to be used on the second day of a two-week trip, no doubt hoped that this daily string of bizarre events would cease. Several boys, oblivious to my warnings about rattlesnakes, plunged into the brush and soon retrieved the tire, which had deflated and come off its rim. Fortunately, it looked fixable, but, in the meantime, it was necessary to mount our sole remaining spare tire.

The 270 miles we traveled that day took eleven hours, including the stop for peanut butter sandwiches and tire repair. We rolled into the municipal park in Boise just as the sun was setting. In my earlier contacts, I had discovered that camping was permitted in a section of this large park. Soon we were cooking dinner by lantern light in the big park shelter. It was a hungry bunch that devoured the stew of canned beef and fresh vegetables. We weren't used to eating at the stylish hour of 9 p.m.!

Because we were late turning in, our morning departure from Boise was not quite so early as the previous day, but we only had 270 miles to drive. From the map, the highway appeared to cross a non-mountainous part of southern Idaho. That day we discovered what we already should have known: The Bus didn't require mountains to be slow! The drop down into the Snake River Valley and, particularly, the climb up to the plateau on the other side, assured another late arrival at our evening campsite. Dorm didn't dare shorten the day's drive and try to find a place to stop earlier because he could see that we would never be able to make up the lost time.

When he could see that after our arrival at camp in Pocatello dinner would be even later than the night before in Boise, he made a bold move. Not wanting to risk Boy Scouts' collapsing from starvation—that didn't take long at the age of these

161

boys—he pulled into a small Idaho city.

He stopped at a bank, got rolls of quarters, and gave each boy one quarter. "You're on your own for dinner, fellows," he told us.

"Wow," we thought, "How great!" There wasn't much choice of places to dine, especially for 25 cents, so most of us crowded into a hamburger place where our coins bought us a hamburger and chocolate shake. They were good shakes, too, beaten from hard ice cream, milk, and chocolate syrup, unlike the stuff coming from machines today that kids think is fine because they've never tasted the real thing.

Dorm was right; we didn't pull into the city park in Pocatello until about 9:30 p.m. We immediately rolled out our sleeping bags, stripped to our underwear, and hit the hay. No horsing around that night; it had been a long day and we dozed off quickly, dreaming of Yellowstone the next day.

I awoke to Bill's exclamation, "My gosh, we're lying right in the city!"

Bill was so right. Our sleeping bags were lying a few feet from a city sidewalk. We were separated by only a chain link fence from the many people bustling along the sidewalk. A row of houses lay directly across the street. Residents were coming and going. Pocatello certainly seemed like a busy town at 7:30 on a Tuesday morning! How were we to get dressed in full view of the populace? By pulling our clothes into our sleeping bags and struggling into them inside the bags, of course. Those whose clothes were not in easy reach stood up, holding the bags around their chests, and hopped over to

162

their pants and shirts.

You'll always find a sleepy head or two when you get so many boys together, and Repete (Pete's younger brother) didn't want to get up. We didn't know whether he was embarrassed or sleepy, and we didn't much care. This called for the usual treatment. Two boys, up and dressed, took hold of the foot end of the bag, lifted it high, and dumped the skivvie-clad lad onto the ground. No place for modesty now . . . . Repete had no choice but to pull on trousers and shirt as quickly as possible in full view of the townspeople who, now that I think about it, didn't seem much interested.

Poor Tom Tyser!

Our fourth day on the road turned out to be a big one. We were on the final stretch to Yellowstone. In early afternoon, The Bus pulled up to the National Park entrance at West Yellowstone. Dorm got out to talk to the park ranger on duty, confident of a warm reception for this fine group of lads from The Home of the Pacific Fleet. A surprise awaited!

The ranger on duty said rather gruffly, "We can't let you fellows in the park."

Dumbfounded, Dorm kept his temper—no mean feat for our leader under such circumstances—and learned the causes of the problem. The ranger felt that our bus might violate the monopoly possessed by the official park buses. Also, a Scout troop from Illinois had just left the park, leaving behind a trail of mayhem and minor vandalism. Dorm did some fast talking and promised exemplary behavior from these flowers of youth from the shores of Puget Sound. Possibly he shed a tear or two over the unfulfilled dream of these young Americans to see the greatest of national parks. He must have gotten through to the ranger. In any case, there was undoubtedly no legal basis for keeping us out. Soon we were rolling on to our camp at Madison Junction.

You can be sure we set up a neat camp and looked our sharpest, even going to the extreme of donning our Scout uniforms. A word from Dorm about the Illinois hoodlums (we felt that these "Back-Easters" should be expelled from the Boy Scouts of America!) was enough to make us want to prove what real Boy Scouts were like.

I think we redeemed Scouting pretty well at the evening campfire program where we sat on log benches, listening to a talk from the ranger. We provided everyone there with some entertainment by way of Scouting songs. With our uniforms and purple-and-gold bandanas we must have been a fine-looking bunch all right.

To warn us about the hazards to come in the thermal areas, the ranger taught us a little song:

> "Little Tom Tyser,
> He slipped in a geyser
> And he began to cry,
> Ma-a! Ma-a!
> Poor little innocent guy."

A pretty dumb song, I thought at the time, but the fact is I still remember it, and not one of us slipped in a geyser at Yellowstone!

164

Our troop spent several magical days in the park. We saw all of the famed Geyser Basins; Old Faithful performed right on schedule for us. We marveled at bubbling paint pots, the long fishing bridge at Lake Yellowstone (the boys had less luck here than later at Heart Lake in the Olympics), the spectacular canyon and waterfalls of the Yellowstone River, the bears alongside the road. The Bus creaked and groaned its way over 9,000 foot Dunraven Pass. We viewed the colorful ter- races at Mammoth Hot Springs; we saw it all. I've visited Yellowstone several times since and have always thrilled at the wonders in this first of our National Parks. But no visit ever quite equaled the delight of this first one in the company of 35 other enthusiastic boys from the little town of Bremerton.

We participated in evening campfires everywhere, got along famously with the park rangers and were given a warm goodbye as we left the park at the Gardiner Gateway in Montana. We knew we had helped redeem the good name of the B.S.A.

Leaving the park was a little sad, but we boys dwelt more on the prospect of fun ahead; we couldn't forsee the special ad- venture that Montana would hold!

The Errant Axle

As we rolled north across the hot prairies toward the Little Belt Mountains on our way to Glacier Park, we paralleled a freight train rolling along through the endless wheat fields. We always made a game of counting the number of cars in the trains, and this train set the record. What a thrill when the last of the 150 freight cars rolled by. Perhaps these trains had a special fascination for us because Bremerton was at the time the largest town in the U.S. without any rail connection. To us this was a disgrace, but it was remedied three years later during World War II when a rail line was extended from Shelton to the Navy Yard.

We stopped to buy a couple of day's provisions in the little frontier town of White Sulfur Springs. Wow! This was the real Wild West. Horses right in town, men wearing cowboy hats. I think we were just a little disappointed that we saw no shoot-out. Dorm purchased several large watermelons. This brought special praise from Bud, who promptly dubbed them our "green chickens." He talked eagerly about having a big piece of green chicken that night. Luckily, no townfolk were close enough to overhear—green chicken really doesn't sound very appetizing!

Soon Dorm shifted into compound low gear as The Bus ground along at about 6 miles per hour on the long climb to the summit of the pine-clad Little Belt Mountains. Because the weather was warm, many of us were taking an afternoon snooze. Suddenly, there was a loud "crack," and the engine of the old Fageol wound up, but we stood still. Dorm knew at once what had happened; a rear axle had snapped!

The immediate problem wasn't too great; we were able to roll back downhill and off the road into a Forest Service campground. Dorm had noticed this place when we crawled passed it five minutes earlier, a half-mile back.

We stopped at a fine spot in the pines beside a rushing stream, and we were delighted to be camping there. Dorm and a couple of the older boys went into a huddle with more serious things on their minds. Here we were, in a remote mountain range 60 miles from the nearest sizable city, Great Falls, with no spare axle. It wasn't really surprising, because who, after all, carries a spare bus axle around with him?

While most of us set up a camp and went about the usual pursuits—a game of touch football, playing in the stream, generally horsing around—Dorm jacked up the rear of The Bus and removed the errant steel shaft. The hub had cleanly broken from it. With a sigh, he and two of the older boys took it out to the roadside and looked for someone to hitch a ride with. Traffic was very light in those days, but people were friendly, and the first car that came along picked up the trio. They learned that there was a mechanic at Neihart, just a few miles away over the summit, so that town became their destination.

I suspect that the mechanic in this mountain hamlet had never faced a broken Fageol bus axle. But he was game to tackle anything and did the best job he could in welding the hub back to the shaft. It took a while for Dorm to flag a car going back toward the camp, and he rolled in just after Reverend Pyle, with the help of a couple of senior boys, had finished preparing our dinner. Darkness fell quickly in the mountains— this was pre-Daylight Savings time—and installation of the axle had to await the morning.

The next day was Saturday and, even as breakfast was being fixed by senior staff, Dorm was slipping in the new axle and bolting the dual tires to it.

"O.K. boys, Let's try 'er out!" Dorm said, as he climbed into the driver's seat.

After a couple of cranks by Johnny, the Fageol roared to life.

We held our breath as Dorm pushed it into gear and nursed the gas pedal.

We cheered as the bus moved a foot or two . . . then groaned as we heard a loud snap. The engine revved up, signalling that the axle had again failed. Dorm emerged with a long face, already thinking of his next step. He knew it wouldn't be feasible for Troop 511 to take up permanent residence in the Little Belt Mountains of Montana. The Montana winters would be too cold for us tidewater kids!

After eating quickly, Dorm and two senior boys were at road-side again, axle in hand, and thumbs extended in the time-honored fashion. They looked for a ride to Great Falls, some sixty miles north. Within a few minutes, a big Army-style truck of the Civilian Conservation Corps (CCC, as this de-pression-era program of national service for young men was universally known) rolled to a stop and picked up the three.

We shouted "Good luck!" as the truck lumbered up the grade and out of sight.

Of course, we didn't hear what happened until a '36 Chevy rolled into our camp before noon the next day with Dorm and the two others. We learned that the CCC truck had deposited them late on Saturday afternoon at an auto supply/mechanics shop in Great Falls known by the CCC fellows. The lone person there—the owner—was wiping his hands with a rag as Dorm's crew entered, broken axle in hand. They briefly ex-plained the situation.

"Well," the amiable Montanan said, "I'm about to close up for the weekend. The missus is having folks over for dinner tonight. But let's see if we've got anything here that will do the trick."

A brief search showed no Fageol bus axle in stock, not a surprising development. However, he did discover a truck axle of the proper dimension. Unfortunately, the holes for the lugs were not of the right size.

With a slight shake of his head, the Montanan said, "Fellows, I think I can drill these so they'll work if you come back first thing Monday morning."

Dorm became his most eloquent self in explaining that the marooned boys probably would starve before then. Wasn't there anything that could be done sooner? Without a word, the mechanic sighed, went to the phone, and told his wife he'd be a little late and to go ahead and start without him. He then proceeded to spend about an hour drilling the holes in the tempered steel to the proper diameter. He accepted payment only for the axle itself, just a few dollars, and told Dorm to consider his labor a donation to the Boy Scouts.

As they were all leaving the shop, Dorm asked the mechanic if he could recommend a place for the three to spend the night. He told them to hop in his car, and he drove them to a nearby motel and introduced them to the owner. With a wave and a hope that the axle would work O.K., the Good Samaritan drove off into the night to the grateful thanks of the 511'ers.

The kindness of Great Falls folks didn't end there. After a worry-free night's sleep, Dorm and the two boys awoke to an offer from the motel owner and his wife to drive them back to the mountain camp. They also offered to let 511 camp on the motel lawn that night. Dorm accepted both offers with gratitude.

The Little Belt saga ended happily early in the afternoon when The Bus, with replacement axle in place and boys filled with peanut butter sandwiches and rather stale bread, moved slowly up the camp road onto the highway. Dorm treated the clutch gingerly as he shifted up one gear, but all was well; the new axle was going to be O.K.! And so it proved for as long as 511 owned the bus.

A Test of Fire

Our night in Great Falls seemed luxurious. While most of us "camped" on the motel lawn, Dorm rented a couple of units, one for Reverend Pyle and himself with several senior boys crammed into the other. We all took turns sharing the showers for our first hot water baths in a week and a half. Before that, plunging into an icy stream was all we had. Though bathing was most definitely not a priority for Boy Scouts of that period, I looked forward to my turn in the shower. When the time came, I eagerly stepped in . . . into an icy waterfall! No motel water heating system could handle 35 consecutive hot showers!

By now we had well established our daily on-the-road routine of sleeping, talking, singing, and reading comic books. A couple of times we had bologna for lunch instead of peanut butter sandwiches, and we considered that a real luxury. We rolled into Glacier National Park and passed muster at the entrance post without a hitch. That notorious Illinois gang apparently hadn't ventured this far north! After a night at a campground near beautiful St. Marys Lake, we slowly climbed

170

up the famed Going-to-the-Sun Highway to Logan Pass. We had never seen a more scenic mountain road. Gazing up at the soaring peaks with their sculpted sides and down to the deep blue of the lake, with waterfalls in between, quieted even our lively bunch. A short hike at the summit to view a glacier brought us back to life.

When we arrived at the viewpoint allowing a vista of the small icefield, we all agreed, "They call that a glacier? It'd fit into one corner of Anderson!"

The observation was more than the voice of local pride; the glaciers in Glacier National Park were small. Still, as the plaque at the site described, they were just remnants of the mighty glaciers that in past centuries carved the great cirques and valleys that certainly were awe-inspiring.

After passing the summit and proceeding down the equally spectacular west side of the pass, we knew that we were heading home. At the rate the Fageol could travel, it would still take several days, but we were heading west toward Bremerton. A third and final flat tire occurred in northern Idaho, resulting in a search for another spare in Spokane. This search ended successfully when Dorm located a tractor tire of the right "caliber," purchased it, and stowed it on top of The Bus. We camped at a state park on the edge of the city, and the next day ground our way across the hot fields and hills of a Washington state July. Of course, air conditioning was something most of us had never heard of, let alone experienced. Open bus windows didn't do much good when the air temperature outside reached nearly 100 degrees.

One great adventure remained for what was supposed to be

171

our last day on the road. We rolled past deserted farmhouses where irrigation waters from Grand Coulee Dam and resulting green fields were still several years in the future. We enjoyed views of the mighty Columbia River, at that time flowing majestically and freely through a lava-sided gorge. We stopped briefly at Ghinko State Park. We gazed at petrified logs and wondered how there ever could have been a forest in this barren landscape. We continued slowly in compound low gear up a dry wash on Highway 10. Then it happened.

I was dozing as the engine of The Bus growled loudly, and the blazing sun heated us all to a pretty pink. I was rudely blasted awake by a cry from the front, "Dorm, the bus is on fire!"

Even the sleepiest of us was awake now, wide-eyed awake. Dorm looked at the crack around the clutch pedal and quickly confirmed Oren's observation; there were flames in the engine compartment.

"Everyone out the windows!" Dorm bellowed as he hit the brakes

No need to repeat that order! I was on the shoulder of the road in three seconds. I noted that no other vehicle was in sight on the long grade and thought, "What a pity. That would have been some sight, seeing a whole load of boys erupt out of the windows of the old bus!"

Dorm opened the engine hood and crisply ordered to the older fellows nearby, "Get dirt!"

With bare hands, canteen cups, whatever was available, the command was obeyed. Dirt flew into the engine compart-

172

ment and, in moments, only a curl of smoke and the acrid smell of burned wire insulation remained.

Dorm looked in and said, "Looks like things got so hot under the hood that old oil on the engine block caught fire. Some of the insulation is charred; hope the wires still work!"

After cooling the engine for a few minutes, Dorm climbed back into the driver's seat and pushed the starter. With a cough or two, the engine roared into life, and we cheered.

Dorm said, "We've got to nurse this thing up to the plateau. It'll be easier on the engine and safer for all of you if you walk along the road until we get there."

So walk we did, in a single file on the shoulder, behind the laboring bus, and under a 100-degree sun. It was only a mile and a half to the top of the grade, but it took more than three-quarters of an hour to reach it. The few cars that passed by must have wondered what we had all done to be banished from The Bus and condemned to walk in that hot sun! I suppose today a passerby would have reported the goings-on, the sheriff would have arrived, and Dorm would be hauled off in handcuffs, accused of child abuse!

Once again, the guardian angel of Troop 511 came through. We all climbed back into The Bus, and it rolled safely on the downgrade to Ellensburg, about 20 miles ahead. Here, some of the dirt was blown away and some wiring replaced at a service station. We resumed our journey several hours late, clearly unable to reach our home destination that night. We camped a final night in a quiet spot alongside the Cle Elum River. Splashing in that water to cool off and remove the sweat and grime of the day felt better than any bath at home!

We had kept folks back home informed by telephone of our progress and delay. We met a considerable greeting party and many happy reunions as we piled out of the old bus at the troop hall in Charleston. I can't verify that this actually happened, but I would be willing to bet that Reverend Pyle looked at his old church when he got out and offered up a "Thank you, Lord!" as he was met by a waiting family.

Chapter 8

MEANWHILE, BACK IN BREMERTON

The Eagles Fly High

Memories of 511 combine the adventure and fun of camping at Tahuya, hiking in the mountains, and going on tours with the hard work and pride involved in being good Boy Scouts, especially a good troop. The fun and the work were fully mixed over the years. I've found that this is always the best way to live.

Until the late 1920s, Charleston, lying west of the original Bremerton, was an incorporated town. That it became a part of the larger city of Bremerton didn't stop use of the name "Charleston." Troop 511 made its home in the basement of the Charleston Baptist Church during the years I was a member. Reverend Pyle of that church, though not seen much at our meetings, was sort of our benevolent Godfather . . . no pun intended. You've already read of his role in defending Dorm's purity in the encounter with the drunken woman at Sacajawea State Park. The boys all liked him, but his main role was in providing a big basement in which our meetings were held.

These Thursday evening affairs were attended by 30 to 60 boys all in colorful Scout uniform, with kerchiefs in the bright—one might say gaudy—511 colors, purple and orange. As Dorm matured as Scoutmaster, the uniforms more and more frequently included merit badge sashes displaying marks of increased accomplishments by the boys—colorful icons of conquests in hiking, swimming, cooking, first aid, and other Scout-

177

ing essentials, supplemented by those in more esoteric fields such as astronomy, chemistry, aeronautics, and pet care. Attainment of five merit badges enabled the First Class Scout to become a Star Scout; ten opened the way to Life rank.

The magic number of 21 merit badges (some of which had to be in specified fields) was the key to attaining the coveted rank of Eagle Scout. Just about everyone in 511 dreamed of becoming an Eagle, a goal instilled by a combination of self-pride and a desire to be thought well of by our respected leaders, Dorm and Bill. At one Court of Honor, five 511 Scouts were awarded their Eagle badges at one time. This stunning accomplishment was easily surpassed in a couple of years when first eight, then later thirteen, boys became Eagles at single Courts of Honor. Altogether fifty 511 Scouts attained Scouting's highest rank, a Kitsap County record.

Let's Win 'Em All!

The boys of 511 were nothing if not proud and self-confident in those days—let's face it, we were cocky! The annual troop inspections by Kitsap District officials were prepared for earnestly. The inspections included a review of troop records and activities, as well as a personal inspection of the troop in full uniform at a regular meeting. During the day or two prior to the annual inspection, cries were heard at 511 homes around town, "Mom! Haven't you sewed on my Animal Husbandry merit badge yet! It's got to be on by Thursday night!" "My Life badge looks like it's on kind of crooked." "Where are my clean knee socks?" Of course, moms would counter, with full justification, "Why didn't you tell me sooner this had to be done right now?"

However, when the big night rolled around, everyone was in good shape. Standing in line for the inspectors, these 12- to 17-year-old boys looked as proud as, and a lot more colorful than, a platoon of U.S. Marines! During my first year with the troop, I remember how eagerly we awaited the results of the inspection. Finally Dorm, with only the slightest show of pride marring his otherwise matter-of-fact demeanor, announced at a meeting that we had taken first place.

Never a group to rest on laurels, we tackled next year's inspection, and the one after that, with increased vigor and determination. Once on top, no one was going to push us off! And they couldn't . . . 511 won top honors three years running. There's no telling how long this would have gone on, because there were no more annual inspections after that. Why? We heard that it was because our continual winning was too discouraging to other troops! Sounded like a reasonable explanation to us . . . but we did think the others were a little "chicken" to quit like that. Of course, there might have been another, less ignoble reason, but, if so, we never heard it.

Then there was the big Field Meet down at City Park one Saturday morning in summer. This brought together all Kitsap troops at one time in a test of various scouting skills. There were ten categories of competition, including such things as knot tying, fire building, first aid, pathfinding, and bird identification (from colored pictures). Fortunately, we didn't think of it as such, but the Field Meet really was just another test like those we disdained at school. Preparation for it took a lot more time than getting ready for annual inspections. Weeks of drilling climaxed at the last Thursday troop meeting before the Meet.

"Gee, Oren, I just can't seem to get the hang of tyin' the bowline!" said a worried Tenderfoot.

"O.K., Buddy. Just pretend this loop in the rope is a lake, then have a fish jump up out of it, go around the back side of the tree, and back into the lake. Tighten it up and you've got a bowline."

It sounded silly, but it was a trick that helped get this classic sailor's knot tied right. And you can be sure on Saturday, Buddy did get it right.
'
We were all fired up on the Saturday of the meet. It was, after all, a big event . . . today, we'd call it the "Super Bowl" of scouting activities.

One of the more exciting events was fire building. Each team was given a little bit of wood, two matches, and a small pan of salted water (the salt lowered the boiling point). The object was to get the water boiling in the shortest amount of time. I was on the 511 fire building team.

Our team was ready, on the blocks, and set to go in what in my imagination was the 1940 Olympics. The starter's whistle sounded, and, with my Scout knife, I began making shavings—fast—from a block of wood. Billy was cutting larger pieces, and Al was arranging these into a neat pyramidal shape with shavings underneath, just as we had practised.

Johnny, our team leader, said, "O.K. guys, I'm going to light up."

We each held our breath as he scratched the precious

matchstick on a stone—once, then twice. A bright yellow flame sputtered into life. Johnny cupped his hand around it as it threatened to die away in the slight breeze. Suddenly it was blazing and he carefully placed it beneath the shavings. Success!

"Now, Al," Johnny said calmly, "put on the can."

Using a small stick provided for the purpose, Al held the can of water over the burgeoning flame, as I carefully added fuel to the flames. I glanced around at neighboring teams. I heard one group groaning; they had just used their second match and it had gone out! I could see flames flickering at other sites, though.

"Come on, come on," I silently pleaded as I continued to stoke our little fire. All at once bubbles began to appear in our water, and then it boiled, really boiled!

The judge watching us shouted "We have a boil!" Within seconds similar cries arose from judges at other teams . . . but there was no doubt about it, ours was first! We'd won a gold medal in those imaginary Olympics!

It was a story repeated many times that day. When the morning was over, Troop 511 had won nine first places in the ten events. Surely this could only be described as a great feat, but most 511'ers felt a twinge of disappointment. Why hadn't we made a clean sweep of it? Probably a little crooked judging on the tenth event (I don't recall which one had eluded us), was the general consensus. Dorm and Bill didn't share any feeling of disappointment, though, and bought celebratory ice cream cones for all our teams, even the one that had been

181

cheated of victory in its event!

Yet another competition lay ahead. Every several years a Camporee was held; the forthcoming one was to be in Bremerton's Forest Ridge Park, which today as then is largely wooded and undeveloped. Patrols from each troop were assigned an area in which to set up camp and spend the night, cooking dinner and breakfast in their campsites. Roving judges compared the way the patrols went about their work; the way the campsites looked; the quality of meals; and the overall spirit, discipline, and Scouting expertise shown. At that time, 511 had five patrols, and, because of our monthly camping experience at Tahuya, plus the summer mountain hikes, we didn't need a whole lot of special practise for the Camporee!

As might be expected, it was another runaway. The Beaver Patrol even showed off a little by baking a big chicken for dinner. These clever Beavers dug a hole, lined it with rocks, built a fire in the hole until the rocks were sizzling hot, removed the fire, placed the seasoned chicken (thoroughly wrapped in cooking parchment and wet leaves) in the hole, covered it with soil and rocks, and then built a fire on top. When I saw this neighboring patrol digging the chicken out, smelled the wonderful aroma, and noted the delighted expression on the judge's face as he bit into a sample, I felt a twinge of envy, mixed with grudging admiration. We had fixed a great beef stew, but, wow! roast chicken in camp . . . that was really something! However, I was happy that it was a 511 patrol that came up with this delight. (I recalled decades later that this method of cooking chicken was similar to treatment of pig at a Hawaiian luau. No 511 boy had ever been anywhere near Hawaii at that point in his life, but perhaps one of them had read about this cooking method.)

182

Apparently that chicken turned the trick . . . the patrol won first place in the Camporee. And other 511 patrols also took second and third prizes. Looking around at the camping efforts of other troops from my very prejudiced perspective, I thought it was a good thing there wasn't a fourth and fifth prize, or we would have taken those too!

Troop 511 had internal competitions between its patrols as well. One involved gathering used paper to raise funds for our 1939 trip, as mentioned previously. My Cougar Patrol went all out on this one. We built a monstrous wagon with high sides that we called the "Cougar Cart" to gather our newspapers. We scoured our end of the city, hauling this wagon about and filling it. Our home had an unfinished basement room, and we just threw the papers in there as we collected.

In a couple of weeks, the room was nearly full to its ceiling. Then the moment of truth came, and we had to sort this amorphous mass of old newspapers into neatly tied bundles. What a job that was . . . just as my mother had warned! The reward came when it was announced that we were top performers in the paper drive and were taken for dinner and some sightseeing in the state capital, Olympia, including a visit to the State Legislature in session.

During another competition, in which the patrols completed projects to gain points in the inter-patrol competition, I decided to make signs for Tahuya. I painted relatively neat highway-type pointer signs, identifying such camp features as Sundown Lodge, Tahuya River, Sims Pond, Boughton Bog, Peterson Pond, and McCaslin Marsh. Most of these reflected names of troop members. Imagine my surprise in much later

183

years to note on offical county maps the name "McCaslin Marsh," right where it should be! My sign must have still been there when some mapmaker surveyed the area.

The reader shouldn't get the feeling that this was pretty much of a "goody-goody" bunch of kids. Even in official Scouting activities there was much horseplay and humor, although pretty innocent by contemporary standards. On one occasion, troops in Bremerton had chartered an old ferryboat to take a large gang to the annual Scout Circus in Seattle. This was great fun . . . our own ferryboat! So what if it was rather small and run down! My principal memory is not of the Circus itself, which was always spectacular, but of the ferry trip and most especially of Bud—the lead joker of our troop—selling hot dogs at a concession stand in the passenger cabin. It was great fun watching him operate.

A boy would step up and say, "A hot dog, please."

Bud would reply, "Sure thing, pal."

He'd slap some mustard and ketchup on the bun, reach into the pot of warm water for a weiner, and hand the hot dog to the hungry boy.

The boy would take a big bite, and then exclaim, "There's no weenie in here!"

Bud would express surprise, look, and say, "What the heck happened to it? You saw me put it in!" After glancing at the floor to see if the boy had dropped the frankfurter, he'd give a patient sigh and put another weiner in the bun and hand it back.

What Bud had done with great verve (and considerable expertise) was to palm the first weiner, quickly place his finger in the bun and pull the bun off and hand it to the victim. As I think about it, it's hard to see how it worked, but work it did, time and again! What a master Bud was! Luckily, there was no health inspector aboard to foil his scheme.

All of our successes in competitions, plus having our own bus and camp, and well-publicized activities such as the Yellowstone-Glacier bus trip, drew boys to 511 like bears to honey. A normal troop has four patrols and about 30 boys. Ours at its peak had seven regular patrols and about 60 boys. We had to use both the bus and Dorm's old truck to take us to Camp Tahuya and other destinations such as Lake Quinault.

Officials of Kitsap District had mixed feelings about this tide of popularity. Of course, it was fine to see a troop thriving with enthusiastic boys rapidly moving ahead through Scouting ranks. However, it was adversely affecting the recruiting efforts of other fine troops in the District . . . and they were fine troops, probably among the best in the Boy Scouts of America at the time. Finally, Dorm reported to us that it had been suggested by someone in authority (we never knew precisely who the villain was) that our troop should be split in two with Bill Juneau heading a spin-off troop. In hindsight, this was a logical idea, since Bill was such a fine leader in his own right. However, it created a storm of protest among 511 Scouts and we heard no more of this dastardly (we thought) scheme.

Where the Fuzzy Marmots Grow

Bill Gets Crab-by

Bill Juneau figured prominently in another story involving several members of Troop 511.

Dorm had decided in 1940 that it was time for a little travel. The Golden Gate International Exposition in San Francisco, that had opened in 1939 for a two-summer run, seemed an attractive destination. So he rounded up my brother Bob and me, Billy, Johnny, and Red, and off we went in the 1940 Nash we borrowed from grandpa.

We were an excited but naive bunch as we headed for California. At our first breakfast stop in Shelton, about 30 miles down the road from Bremerton, Billy and I ordered cinnamon rolls.

The waitress asked us, "How about it, boys? Want those cinnamon rolls heated?"

That sounded good to us so we told her to go ahead. A few minutes later she brought two plates, saying "Here you go, fellows. Enjoy your rolls!"

We looked at the rolls, then at each other. "Glad she blew out the flames," Billy said.

To say that the rolls had been heated was like saying that Mount Rainier was little frosty in January. They were charred black! Still, we didn't know enough to complain but ate a few dark-brown bites out of the center of each and went on our way, sadder though not too much wiser.

186

A day later, after a lunch stop at a northern California cafe, Billy came running out to Dorm as he was about to get into the Nash, handed him some coins, and said, "Dorm! You left this money on the table!" We small-town lads had not yet learned about the worldly custom of tipping!

We finally arrived in "Frisco," as we called it then, and had a grand old time seeing all the sights at the exciting world's fair. Well, not quite all . . . Dorm wouldn't let us go into Sally Rand's Nude Ranch!

We were sorry that Bill Juneau wasn't with us, that he was still toiling away in the Navy Yard. While visiting Fishermen's Wharf on the city's waterfront, Red had an inspiration.

"Let's send Bill a present," he said, and there was agreement all around.

"How about one of those great crabs!" Johnny went on.

So together we ponied up the fifty cents or so that a big crab fresh from boiling water cost in those days. The fish peddler boxed and wrapped the crab for us. Now, I mentioned that we were naive. However, we weren't stupid. We knew that a freshly cooked crab wouldn't ship well. In fact, to make sure that it wouldn't we let it sit on the porch of our South San Francisco motel while we visited the fair the next day. Yes, the famed California sun was shining and it was warm!

The following day we mailed the package to Bill in Bremerton.

When we returned home a few days later we couldn't wait to hear how Bill enjoyed his "gift." It turned out our prank worked almost too well. Bill said that several days after we had mailed the package, a postman approached his house holding a package by its string, dangling on the end of a long stick. Cats for blocks around must have been lifting their noses, because the stench was terrible. Bill told us the mailman simply said, with a masterpiece of understatement, "Please tell your friends not to send fresh food through the mail. We put this package in a corner, but the entire post office stank anyway before I could start my rounds today!"

I hope we had at least a twinge of regret about the distress we caused innocent workers, but I fear our delight that we had pulled a good one on Bill was the dominant emotion!

Life Gets Real

As Bremerton moved toward 1941, the world scene began to intrude on Scouting life. I vividly recall listening to radio accounts of the fall of France and the impending Battle of Britain during a 1940 summer stay at the Seattle Area Council's Camp Parsons. In Bremerton, with its great naval base, we perhaps were more aware of these events than kids in other locales.

As the U.S. moved into a stage of military buildup in 1941, the troop was inevitably affected.

A Marine sergeant named Carson, based in the Navy Yard and himself a former Boy Scout, began attending troop meetings. He soon had us drilling in self-defense using six-foot long staves. A few skinned knuckles didn't deter "Sarge," as he shaped up our formations with a little close order drilling. This was no mean feat in the rather tight quarters of our meeting hall! Our favorite order always was, "Fall out!" signifying the end of the drill.

Then a group of the older 511 boys began training with the Bremerton Fire Department as an auxiliary force to be used in the event of air raids. It was exciting to learn how to attach fire hoses to hydrants, hold the hoses, and put water on target. We found that those hoses really had a kick-back, and, more than once, we got inadvertently sprayed by a loose hose.

Then came that Sunday morning forever etched in the minds of those old enough to remember.

A young neighbor lady whose husband was a sailor on a heavy cruiser in the Pacific ran into our house, crying "The Japs are bombing Pearl Harbor!" And we all knew instinctively that our lives were changed forever.

Bremerton had practise blackouts earlier that year. Although the actual Pearl Harbor attack was certainly a shock, people in Bremerton had been mentally preparing for war with Japan for several years.

And now we entered in earnest into a period of blackouts. On the night of December 7 when no one knew if the Japanese were about to strike at the West Coast, the 511 auxiliary firefighters reported to the main station and held another drill, this time with a lot less bantering and horseplay. We were at war, and we were willing to do our part. Let the bombers come . . . we'd help put out any fires! Fortunately, Bremerton never was attacked and "doing our part" came later in many ways, including individual military service for most of us.

I've mentioned a number of times the quality of our leadership and, indeed, Dorm and Bill were keys to our success. However, the boys of the troop must share in the credit. These Depression-era youth were resilient and tough and had a lot of smarts. At a mid-1990s reunion of many of the 511 "kids," the qualities that took the troop to the pinnacle of achievement were still apparent. These men had accomplished much, first during World War II (when we lost one of our finest boys), then in higher education, and, finally, in the rough and tumble of life.

But back to earlier days. The summer mountain hikes perhaps epitomized the best of Troop 511, and it's fitting that I conclude with an account of the last such hike I participated in and, I believe, the very best one.

Chapter 9

THE LAST HIKE

The 1939 bus trip had been a marvelous experience--at least for the boys. Dorm, who had to nurse the old bus along for 2,500 miles, might have had a little less enthusiasm. However, we all looked forward to returning to the Olympics in 1940. Indeed, Dorm and Bill were busy planning shortly after the first of the year. They outlined for us a somewhat similar route to the 1937 hike, but in reverse direction with a major variation in its middle. The plan was to start on the Skokomish, go up over First Divide to a base camp at Home Sweet Home, and then across the Duckabush to another base at Heart Lake. Thence, we would hike by a minor path to Anderson Pass and, ultimately, down the Dose.

The wonderful weather we had enjoyed on the two previous hikes supported use of the same period at the end of July, and, when D-Day came, the sun was indeed out in full force as the truck and cars set out along the Canal and Lake Cushman. As we rolled past Staircase camp, I caught a glimpse of the trailhead for Wagonwheel Lake and smiled inwardly, knowing that no one would have to carry me on a trail now!

The first day's hike was just a warm-up, a two-mile jaunt on almost level grade to Big Log camp. This was set in a superb grove of huge virgin timber—mostly Western Red Cedar and Douglas Fir—beside an especially beautiful stretch of the Skokomish River. I again indulged in that favorite pastime, daydreaming by a whitewater section. I saw imaginary river ports, roads linking them across the damp sand bars, and brave pilots taking their craft out into the swirling, dashing waters.

After a time, I noted a perfect place to re-channel a small part of the large river—no danger here of repeating the Jello fiasco at Home Sweet Home! Bill and Bob joined me on this damming endeavor, and soon we saw new land suitable for more imaginary cities emerge from formerly flooded lands.

The next day we passed Camp Pleasant (no one dared remind Dorm of the pea soup problem of the earlier summer), and, finally, we were grinding up the First Divide. Even with leg and knee problems from coming down the passes, going up was indeed harder. It took quite a few "blows" to get there, but, in early afternoon, we were on top with just a short, easy walk down to Home Sweet Home. This camp was as beautiful as we remembered it; the wildflowers in the meadow stretched out probably a quarter mile from the shelter.

We had perfect weather for our day and two nights at Home Sweet Home. Bill Juneau and a group of older kids headed out early for a hike up Mount Steel across the valley, while Dorm led the rest of us up nearby Mount Hopper, an easier climb than the challenging Mount Steel. We found an easy back way by a rough trail to its summit. From the top though, we gazed—carefully—down the virtually vertical cliffs that dropped off toward our camp. The outstanding view spread before us in all directions, and it was a great feeling to have climbed a real mountain, one named on all the maps!

Mabel, Beautiful Mabel!

Our next camp, at Heart Lake, required dropping down into the Duckabush Valley and a good climb back up the other side. This glorious spot was one of the most beautiful campsites of any that we found on 511's summer hikes. As lakes in

194

the high Olympics go, it was fairly good-sized, and the far end from our campsite featured sheer rock cliffs rising several hundred feet about the lake surface. We camped on a little knoll near the lake's outlet, a small stream that plunged crazily down in its quest to reach the Duckabush. We were almost at timber line, with only small alpine evergreens around. However, few hikers visited the lake, and there was plenty of dead wood and branches lying about for cooking fires and the evening campfires.

There were trout in the lake and a few of the boys who had rudimentary fishing gear (as rudimentary as bent pins and string in some cases!) had good luck. This led to a situation that we who knew Dorm best (and I guess my brother Bobby and I were at the top of that list!) found mind-boggling. Dorm ate a fish! Now that may not sound very remarkable, especially for a Puget Sounder, but Dorm was an individualist. An unfortunate experience with stomach upset when he was seven years old, so we had been told, had led to a passionate dislike of eating anything that lived in water, salt or fresh. Whenever we had salmon, or crab, or tuna at home, mother cooked hamburger for Dorm.

Bear in mind, we had been several days without fresh food. The trout, cooked briefly in a bit of canned butter, was the most ambrosial fish I had ever tasted. The cold, clear water lent a true sweetness to the flesh. We finally prevailed upon Dorm to try some of the trout. Perhaps the thinner air at that altitude had affected his normally keen—and stubborn—intellect, because after chewing on a morsel he said that it tasted pretty good! I hasten to add that this represented no long-term breakthrough. Dorm never again, knowingly, ate seafood. (Years later he ate a bowl of Manhattan Clam Chowder

195

not knowing what it was, but that's another story!)

One night, our patrol was lying under the stars in our sleeping bags with a small campfire burning at our feet. We talked quietly, the beauty of the night sky hushing the usually noisy horseplay of boys. It was just that kind of place. Eventually we all dropped off. Waking at dawn, we were jolted to find that Red's sleeping bag had worked its way down the slight slope during the night. Usually that wouldn't have been a problem; we often ended up some distance from where we went to sleep. This time, though, the foot of his sleeping bag ended up in the embers of the little campfire. The fire got the best of it, charring several inches of Red's bag at its bottom and burning a hole clear through in one place. We kidded him about what a sleeper he was to snooze right through a king-size hot-foot! Fortunately, the embers didn't actually get to flesh, but Red had a problem at night with cold feet during the rest of the hike.

Meals were always true highlights of the day. I recall the pro-digious effort Dorm and his senior staff made at Heart Lake, cooking dozens of pancakes in big skillets over an open fire and keeping them warm in covered kettles close to the heat. How great a stack of them tasted, covered with syrup made on the spot from sugar, water, and maple flavoring. Add a tin cup of hot cocoa and a strip or two of fried bacon (carried in canned form), and each Scout was well fueled for a busy day. That kind of eating washed away any resentment over the weight of food in our packs.

A recent experience vividly brought back a highlight of our Heart Lake stay. I was reading a fine book about hiking in the Olympics (*Trail Country* by Robert L. Wood) and noted the following in a chapter about the Duckabush: "O'Neill Pass . . . lies between Mount Duckabush and a low peak to the northwest."

With a start I exclaimed, "Why, that's Mount Mabel! What does he mean calling it 'a low peak'?"

Yes, Mount Mabel! And realistically the description of a 'low peak' is apt. But what memories it has!

. . . . . . I promised our expedition leader I wouldn't go far or be gone long as I started my solo climb up the steep slope strewn with boulders and shale. The view down to Heart Lake and nearby meadows and peaks increasingly impressed me as I climbed. At the top, probably 300 feet in elevation above the lake, I took my own "blow" and sat on a rock and savored the fine outlook and a bit of quiet time by myself.

I soon got up, turned my back to the lake, and lost all view of the camp and the other men. I was now a lone mountaineer, facing the hazards of the Himalayas by myself. I was on a broad, rocky plateau that sloped gently upward toward a distant peak standing sharply against a blue sky. Crossing a small ridge, I faced a great unnamed glacier. I well knew the danger of crossing uncharted glaciers alone but had no choice but to press on. After what seemed an endless period, I sighed with relief as I reached the far side of the white mass. The peak now loomed close-at-hand. Its north face presented a sheer wall of rock, unscalable without needed equipment which I didn't have. I felt the curse of a low-budget expedition but, undeterred, hiked on ahead to survey the back side of the peak.

Voila! I spotted a narrow strip of less severe slope between

197

the looming rocks. "Courage!" I told myself, "You can do it!" After a short struggle, I found my self standing atop a previously unscaled peak in the Himalayas. The pangs of hunger attacked me viciously, and I realized it would be fool-hardy to tarry. Besides, I needed to share knowledge of my feat with other members of the party who were anxiously waiting back at the lake. Cautiously I retraced my steps and, at the point of utter exhaustion, staggered into camp, giving a "thumbs up" sign. With a cheer and shouts of "Well done!" and "Good show, old man!" they helped me sit down on a rock and waited eagerly to hear of the conquest . . . . . .

That's a bit like I felt at the time although reality fell far short of imagination. I had to cross a modest snowfield, and I dis-covered that the north face of the small peak was sheer. The back side, however, was just meadow sloping up to the sum-mit, and the "conquest" was surely nothing to write home about. Not so the view, however. Heart Lake, in a deep pocket, could not be seen. I looked down on O'Neill Pass and the broad trail leading up to it. Beyond the pass rose Mount Steel with its perpetual snowfields, and to the west of the pass stretched the vast Quinault Valley, the deepest and longest in the Olympics. Turning the other way I enjoyed a splendid view of a glacier-girt peak I recognized as Mount Anderson. There's no doubt the wonder of the scene was enhanced by the fact that I was enjoying it alone, from a peak that, although simple to climb, was quite remote. Probably few hikers, if any, had ever stood on it before.

Several of the fellows were excited to hear about my trek, and the next day, with six or seven other boys in tow, I re-peated the climb. A couple of the larger Scouts were bold enough to scramble up the more precipitous side of "my peak," and one of them promptly dubbed it "Mount Mabel" for some obscure reason that has (perhaps happily) faded from memory. We erected a cairn on the summit and entered our names and the date in a tin can with screw top. We made sure that the event would be preserved for posterity!

"I'm Sorry, Ladies!"

Leaving Heart Lake was a bittersweet experience. I was happy to get on to our next adventure, but down inside I knew I was leaving a place that would always be special to me, and one that I would quite likely never see again. But Boy Scouts don't spent a whole lot of time with such philosophizing. Soon we were on the trail once more, our packs a little lighter now.

We passed a lovely little lake called LaCrosse; in later years I've seen it in pictures illustrating the beauty of the Olympics. We then crossed a small ridge and began a drop down to the main trail which leads up from the Quinault River's Enchanted Valley. What a trail that was—really nothing much more than an elk track. The switchbacks came so frequently, and the stretches of trail between each sharp turn were so short, that our thirty boys were strung out over thirteen of the switchbacks at one time. Because it was a warm day in the clear mountain air, all of us were grateful we were going downhill and not up.

Eventually, we reached the broader tread of the main Quinault Trail and headed up toward Anderson Pass. In this area, we had an experience—repeated several times on Olympic hikes—that made life in the high country seem pretty special.

As I trudged along silently, a whispered word came down the line, "Shh! Watch for marmot on the left!"

199

And sure enough, as the troop filed soundlessly by, there stood a large furry marmot on his hind legs on top of a rock about three feet from trail's edge. We had caught him unaware as the head of the line rounded a bend. I guess he decided that if he "froze" we'd just think he was a rock or stump and leave him alone. Troop 511 discipline won the day. We trudged past, glancing furtively to the side in wonder. He stayed in place until the last boy passed, then scampered off into the rocks, grateful to have escaped unharmed from this strange group of bipeds.

As the trail approached the last steep wall of the pass, there were several more switchbacks, but this trail was suitable even for pack horse travel. We seasoned hikers strode ahead easily and soon stood again by the little ponds at Anderson Pass. It was just a short drop down to Camp Siberia where we experienced that great lighter-than-air feeling when we dropped our packs to the ground.

Since we had spent several days at this camp the previous year, we only planned a one-night stop. It would have been unmemorable except for one thing; we finally had a night of the renowned Olympic Peninsula rain. This was the only rainy night we experienced in the three nine-day hikes I was part of, but when the clouds rolled in as we bedded down, followed shortly by the first drops of rain, Dorm knew something had to be done. Not all of us had pup tents and even those boys who had them lacked end flaps. Dorm could see that it was going to be a wet experience unless he took bold action. And he did!

He strode over to the sturdy forest shelter nearby. We had

noted that two women hikers occupied it. These women were real pioneers. Such a sight was unprecedented for us at the time—women deep in the heart of the Olympics!

However, what had to be done had to be done, and Dorm said, "I'm sorry, ladies. I've got thirty boys out here who are getting wet, and we're just going to have to impose ourselves on your hospitality!"

In truth, there didn't seem to be a strong sense of "hospitality," but all of us with inadequate protection—there must have been twenty or so—crowded into the open-ended shelter and put our bags on the floor. The women stayed in two of the wood slab bunks, but we took up every bit of space otherwise; in fact, there was quite a bit of overlapping of sleeping bags.

Still, after the hike of the day, no one had much trouble sleeping. I can't say the sleep was dreamless because, in the middle of the night, several of us heard a sleeping Bud suddenly call out, "Dorm, if I had a pound of jerky I'd cut myself off a chunk and float down the river!"

With that brief but plaintive cry Bud resumed his snoring. He disclaimed any knowledge of the event the next morning so we were denied the full story of his river-floating saga. With rain beating on the roof of our shelter all night and the small headwaters stream of the West Fork of the Dose roaring just outside, the sound effects certainly were right to induce a river-floating dream.

In the gray dawn, we thanked the bemused women who forever after could tell friends how they had slept with twenty young men one night in the mountains. Then we cooked and ate a soggy breakfast outside. It was still quite early when we were on the trail to the Dose Forks camp.

The weather cleared as we left Siberia and passed through Honeymoon and Diamond Meadows. We approached the Dose Forks camp knowing that we would be greeted by more women: this time older members of the Girl Scout troop headed by Helen Juneau, Bill's wife. And there they were. But most of us (except, perhaps, the oldest boys) did our best to ignore them. This proved hard to do after we ate our dinner, when, using a skillet over the open fire, the girls cooked fried pies for everybody. Canned peaches wrapped in pie crust and fried in hot oil seemed about as good as anything we'd ever tasted. Probably eight days on the trail heightened the level of our appreciation, not only of the food, but also of the girls. Even I had to admit, they didn't look too bad by that time.

I had a bit of a surprise on the morning of our last day. I was lying in my sleeping bag in as soft a spot as possible on the forest floor when I awoke with a start. I sensed some movement! I slowly opened my eyes, and, on my bag about six inches from my nose and staring straight at me, was a small field mouse. When my eyes opened—wide!—the little critter paused for just a moment and then scurried off into the brush. He made an effective if unusual alarm. Soon I was struggling to get dressed inside the sleeping bag—you never could tell where those pesky Girl Scouts might be.

After breakfast, Dorm told each of us to put on his most presentable clothing (a difficult choice after so many days of living out of a pack in the wilderness), wash his hands and face, brush his teeth, and comb his hair. We would, after all, be meeting families at the end of the road, and 511 was not only a hardy bunch, but we also could live up to the Scout Law dealing with cleanliness!

We bade good-bye to the girls who headed up the river for a couple more days. Then we started on the last two miles of our nine-day adventure. The walking now was easy, and time passed quickly as we began to sing scouting songs, more-or-less together.

As we sang, eagerly anticipating the feast that always awaited us at the end of the road, my thoughts slipped back to the previous night's campfire. I had enjoyed more than ever before singing the song that always ended our campfires:

> Softly dims the light of day,
> As our campfire fades away.
> Silently each Scout should ask,
> Have I done my daily task?
> Have I kept my honor bright?
> Can I guiltless face the night?
> Have I done and have I dared
> Everything to be prepared?

I knew that each of us could answer "yes" to these questions as we approached the end of the last hike I would ever take with this wonderful bunch.

Chapter 10

EPILOGUE

Dorm Braman left Bremerton and Troop 511 in 1943 when he joined the U.S. Navy. He ended his naval career three years later, after serving in Washington, D.C., as chief of lumber procurement for the Navy with the rank of Commander. His career thereafter included ownership of a thriving building materials business in suburban Seattle, ten years service on the Seattle City Council, a five year term as Mayor of Seattle, which was interrupted by his appointment as Assistant Secretary of the U.S. Department of Transportation (DOT) in Washington, D.C.

His work at DOT focussed on the environment, and he had a major role in promoting mass transit and in preventing damage to mountain areas and urban parks from proposed highways. Upon his return to Seattle, he served as President of the Chief Seattle Council of the Boy Scouts of America. He died in 1980, still an active hiker and avid skier.

I know little of the history of Troop 511 after 1943. Bill Juneau became Scoutmaster that year, and continued until 1949. Several other men led the troop until its dissolution in 1956, which came partly as a result of difficulty in maintaining outdoor activities. Sundown Lodge remained the site of many Kitsap District activities for several years thereafter.

Bill Juneau retired from about 40 years of service at the Puget Sound Naval Shipyard where he served in the important role of Chief of the Allowance Branch in the design department. He died in 1987. His son, Bill, in 1997 became Assistant Council Commissioner for the Chief Seattle Council of the Boy Scouts of America after four years of service as District Commissioner for the Chief Kitsap District.

Although inevitably many Troop 511 "graduates" of the late 1930's and early 1940's moved around the country, a surprising number remained in the region of their Scouting days, the Pacific Northwest. Some remain friends and get together from time-to-time; reminiscing about the 511 days is always a feature of these times.

In 1995, when talking with my closest boyhood friend and neighbor, Bill Gates, the idea of a major reunion of old Scouting friends was born. (If the friend's name sounds familiar, there's a good reason; Bill is the father of the Microsoft president.)

On May 10 of that year, 27 of our contemporaries got together at the beautiful Gates' place on Hood Canal in plain sight of our beloved Olympic Mountains. Most had wives with them, and Helen Juneau, Bill's widow, was an honored guest. Many of the "boys" had brought old photographs and other memorabilia, and what discussions there were among people, some of whom had not seen each other for more than 50 years! Men came from all over the Northwest and California; one guest, a resident of New York, flew in from London for the reunion.

After dinner, each former Scout stood and told what he had been doing for the past 55 years . . . in three minutes each! They told of military service in every branch including the merchant marine; of college degrees attained; of long-lasting, loving marriages; of raising children; of successful careers in the broadest possible range of activities. We heard from a true cross-section of those who built a great America in the post-war years; from a top-ranked corporate attorney, an aerospace engineer, a businessman who built a thriving lumber operation, an electronic engineer, a prominent surgeon, a Boy Scout executive, a dynamic salesman, a Naval Academy graduate, a planning director for two major U.S. cities, a noted fabric designer with a world-wide clientele, and others who had had satisfying, prosperous careers and were now enjoying retirement.

A common thread ran through the brief but inspiring stories we heard: each person had memories of the 511 experience etched in his mind. They all credited this experience with playing a major role in building discipline, in goal-setting, in setting a framework for good citizenship.

As one man said, "I owe a lot to the Boy Scouts and to Dorm Braman and Bill Juneau. I may have forgotten some of the details of what I learned in those years, but the precepts have stayed with me!"

There could be no finer last words for Troop 511 of Bremerton --long gone, still crystal clear in memory-- and for its splendid leaders, Dorm Braman and Bill Juneau.

DORM BRAMAN (left) and BILL JUNEAU (right)
Scoutmaster and Assistant Scoutmaster, circa 1939

THE AUTHOR

James D. Braman is a native of Bremerton, Washington, where he was an Eagle Scout in Troop 511. He received a degree in Civil Engineering from the University of Washington and an MS in Regional Planning from the same school. He is a member of Phi Beta Kappa, Sigma Xi, and Tau Beta Pi honorary societies.

He served three years in the U.S. Army during World War II, attaining the rank of captain in the Transportation Corps.

His professional career in city planning included seven years as Director of Planning for Denver, Colorado, six years as Director of Community Development for Seattle, Washington, and fifteen years as a planning consultant. He received a number of honors during his forty years of full-time employment.

He has written for many publications, including *Traffic Quarterly* and *Rocky Mountain Crossings*. He has been featured speaker for meetings of local and national organizations. *Where the Fuzzy Marmots Grow* is his first book; he has plans for a second in the near future.

INDEX OF MAJOR PLACES IN BOOK
(In Washington State unless otherwise indicated)

211

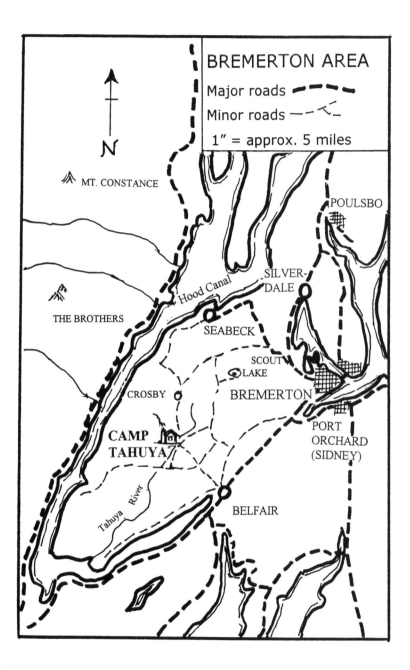

BREMERTON AREA

Major roads

Minor roads

1″ = approx. 5 miles

MT. CONSTANCE

POULSBO

SILVER-DALE

Hood Canal

THE BROTHERS

SEABECK

SCOUT LAKE

CROSBY

BREMERTON

CAMP TAHUYA

PORT ORCHARD (SIDNEY)

Tahuya River

BELFAIR

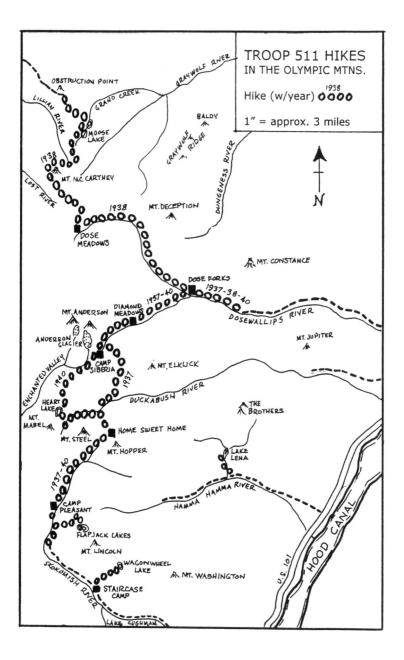

TROOP 511 HIKES
IN THE OLYMPIC MTNS.

Hike (w/year) OOOO ^{1938}

1" = approx. 3 miles

N

OBSTRUCTION POINT
GRAND CREEK
GRAYWOLF RIVER
LILLIAN RIVER
BALDY
MOOSE LAKE
GRAYWOLF RIDGE
1938
MT. McCARTNEY
LOST RIVER
DUNGENESS RIVER
1938
MT. DECEPTION
DOSE MEADOWS
MT. CONSTANCE
DOSE FORKS
1937-38-40
1937-40
DOSEWALLIPS RIVER
MT. ANDERSON
DIAMOND MEADOWS
MT. JUPITER
ANDERSON GLACIER
CAMP SIBERIA
ENCHANTED VALLEY
1937
MT. ELKLICK
1940
DUCKABUSH RIVER
HEART LAKE
THE BROTHERS
MT. MABEL
MT. STEEL
HOME SWEET HOME
MT. HOPPER
LAKE LENA
1937-40
HAMMA HAMMA RIVER
CAMP PLEASANT
FLAPJACK LAKES
MT. LINCOLN
WAGONWHEEL LAKE
MT. WASHINGTON
STAIRCASE CAMP
SKOKOMISH RIVER
HOOD CANAL
U.S. 101
LAKE CUSHMAN

215